FOR THIS CHILD
I HAVE PRAYED

6 Heart Surgeries, 18 Months

R.L. SHAWVER

ISBN: 978-1-637921-14-2 (Hardback)
ISBN: 978-1-637921-15-9 (Paperback)

Library of Congress Control Number: 2021915151

 Published by: Beyond Publishing
BEYOND Beyondpublishing.net

Follow me at www.RLShawver.com
Cover art by James Cornette www.cornfu.com
Website design by Kevin Vertucio hello@enjoytheflite.com
Edited by Toni Shuppe tshuppe@protonmail.com

Ordering Information:
Quantity sales. Special discounts are available on quantity purchases by corporations, associations, and others. For details, contact the publisher at the address above.

Orders by U.S. trade bookstores and wholesalers. Please contact Big Distribution: Tel: (800) 800-8000; Fax: (800) 800-8001 or visit www.bigbooks.com.

Printed in the United States of America

CONTENTS

PREFACE

I saw a quote recently by Morgan Harper Nichols that said,

"Tell the story of the mountains you climbed.
Your words could become a page in
someone else's survival guide."

This was the final point of inspiration I needed to start writing. I spent a lot of time in the hospital with my son. While I was there, I often heard parents say that they felt helpless. When I read others' stories of hospital visits, I find the same lament. "What can we do? We feel so helpless. There's no person or thing to fight, just this invisible sickness."

That wasn't my experience.

I personally don't believe that we are helpless. I believe that there are very powerful weapons of war that we have been given to stand and fight against the forces of darkness that attempt to destroy the beautiful and good things in our lives. I was blessed with incredible mentors in my life who taught me how to fight. The battle came into my home when Samuel was born with two heart defects. Because of the teachings and stories of my mentors, I was familiar with those weapons. When it came time for my fight, they coached me through my battles.

You are not helpless either, but you can't do it alone. There is a God in heaven who has offered to fight our battles for us, and who has offered to partner with us in battle. This book is my account of how God trained me for spiritual warfare.

I pray two things for you as you read this book: I pray you gain a deeper understanding of the how passionately God loves you, and I pray that you can gain insight into the power that He has made available to you. I also hope I can encourage you to seek with greater intensity the God who heals all our diseases.

When it comes to healing, I don't have all the answers. My experience with Samuel's health challenges didn't reveal every aspect of how God works when he heals someone. I have friends who have told me about miracles of God's healing power where limbs grow back, bones deformed from birth are straightened, diseases are cured, cancer is removed, and people are raised from the dead. All of these are stories of instantaneous miracles.

We did not get to experience that with Samuel. Our experience was a different type of miracle, the miracle of conquering struggles inch by inch. I find that I often fail to label these as supernatural, or as miraculous. They aren't quick stories to tell. It is sometimes difficult to see God working clearly. Yet they are miracles no less. Just as God gives us the power to make money, God also gives doctors the insight and the wisdom to heal. He also bridges the gaps that many people take for granted – things like orchestrating the right person in the right place at the right time or keeping my son safe when he had accidents.

To this day, I am still analyzing all that happened to us, but more importantly, I want to stress a core belief of mine: I am not any more special to God than you are. His love for you, and the miracles He wants to do in your life are as many, if not more, than what He wants to do in mine.

If you are reading this book, and you are not what most people would call a Christian, or this sounds like something closer to a fantasy, I want to take a quick moment and welcome you. My life has been radically changed by a relationship with God, and this was only made possible by His son Jesus. Many of the principles that make up my core beliefs may be unfamiliar to you, and the power of which I speak may be far from your understanding. The basis of all this stems from a personal relationship that I have with God. I want to welcome you to start there. If you flip to the end of this book, I'll walk you through the basics. If you would rather read through the book and then come to a decision on a relationship with God later, you know where to find it.

With that said, I want to round this out by speaking directly to anyone who has lost a child or a loved one, especially those who are Christians.

First, my heart aches for you. I also want to tell you that God's heart aches for you.

Second, I really do not have all the answers, but I have a suspicion that as you read, some of my beliefs may challenge yours. Some of the things I state may directly contradict some of the conclusions you have drawn about life and faith and God. I worry about hurting you more, because I know the logical conclusions to which you might arrive. You might think that you could have done more or that you are somehow at fault. You are not at fault. The main premises I have learned from studying the Bible are these: we are at war, and we live in a world that is under the control of the enemy. The enemy comes to steal, to kill, and to destroy. He also comes to lie and manipulate. Satan is the one responsible for the death of your child or loved one, and no other. The main reason I wanted to write this book is this: we are in combat behind enemy lines.

Third, I know that despite what you may think, God is for you and loves you. He is not against you. He did not take your child away from you, even though your child is with Him now. I think you know that as well. If you don't know that, I can tell you from my studies and from the time I have spent getting to know God, that He is not the angry God who takes away children and loved ones. Forgive me for speaking so boldly, but I sense some of you need to hear that.

Understanding that God wasn't punishing me was a key element that kept me going on my journey with Samuel, and what kept me strong. I pray that you come to understand God's place, and your place, and the devil's place in all your circumstances. It's crucial to know who your friends are, as well as your enemies.

I'm going to be bold in this story where I need to bold. It was Reinhard Bonnke who said, "The Gospel is a gospel of power, or it is nothing at all." I typically try to be very gentle, but if you have come to this book in need, dealing with an illness, you don't need gentleness when you are desperate for truth. I ask your permission, as you read, to speak boldly and plainly with you.

INTRODUCTION

My second oldest son, the first son of my wife Stephanie, had six heart surgeries in his first eighteen months of life. Samuel was born with two heart defects that worked against each other.

When he was first fully diagnosed at one month old, one of the doctors in charge of Samuel's health told my wife that if he had been born 30 years earlier, there would have been they could have done. They would have sent him home and told us to spend as much time with him as possible. It dawned on us that this was their gentle way of telling us that Samuel would have died as an infant.

Because of Samuel's heart issues, we had to run to the hospital at least once a month under emergency circumstances. Sometimes the trips were much more frequent. It was an incredibly difficult period of our life, especially since nothing happens in a vacuum. We had a lot of life outside of the hospital that needed to be managed as well. This book is our story, told from my perspective. It is also the story of God's journey with us.

At this point, I want to take a moment and recap some important parts of my life and my faith journey to help you understand my foundation and where I was when Samuel was born.

I decided to give my life to Christ at 15 years old. I had actually grown up in the church. I had even chosen to go forward for an altar call at 6 years old. It wasn't until I was 15 that I made an actual decision to give my life to Christ one August morning.

The spring prior to that summer, there was a girl I sat next to in my 8th grade literature class who wore a jean-skirt to school every day. After a week or two of her wearing skirts every day, when all of the other girls were wearing shorts or jeans, I decided to ask one of my friends. A buddy informed me that it was due to her particular church. In that same year, I was hanging out with friends who had begun to dabble in witchcraft. They often discussed it and would attempt rituals in class when we had free time. I only had a few friends at my high school. I wasn't actively participating in what they were doing, but I was watching intently. There was something about the power of it that appealed to me.

The girl in the jean skirt sat near us and was often privy to many of our conversations and their activities. I fully expected her to be afraid of what my friends were doing. To my surprise, this girl in the jean skirt was unfazed by my friends' demonic pursuits. It's not that she thought there was nothing to it. She wasn't naïve. She just didn't think that what we were doing would have any power over her. She knew she was protected by God. I was intrigued.

Her confidence and commitment to her faith challenged my world view. As the school year ended and summer began, I decided I was going to do what she did. After all, I had grown up in church. For whatever reason, I thought that being a Christian and getting right with God meant living "right." At the age of 10, I had started swearing at the to look cool. That didn't seem like a Christian thing, so I decided to quit that. I spent much of the summer trying to live the best I could and trying to listen for God's voice. I can tell you from experience, trying to be good on your own willpower is exhausting … and fruitless. By August, I was frustrated with my inability to do good, to stop bad habits, and to live righteously.

On the first Monday of August, I woke up early feeling anxious. My dad had been urging me to run and get ready for football practice that August. I went the entire summer not making time for it and now, on the first morning of practice, I felt so convicted for not running that I decided that morning to get up and run.

I laced up a pair of black work boots and took off running. I sprinted up the gravel road towards the small cemetery behind my parents' house. Unsurprisingly, after the first fifty yards, it turned more to walk than run. Still, I returned sweaty and feeling accomplished for attempting to be obedient.

As I removed the uncomfortable boots, I noticed that my sweat on the black leather of my boots had stained my white socks grey. My dad had insisted that I not stain my socks since childhood. This caused a significant amount of guilt over my stained socks. The accomplished feeling of being obedient gave way to more anxiety.

I took my socks off and attempted to get the stains out in the kitchen sink. It was before 8 a.m., and no one else was awake in the house. I sat in front of the kitchen sink scrubbing the socks against each other with dish liquid, trying desperately to get out the black that had worn off of my boots. To my dismay, the black die wasn't coming off with soap.

I rinsed the socks in the kitchen sink, hoping that maybe the running water would take the stains out. I repeated the process a second time, and then a third. The more I scrubbed, the more the guilt continued to grow … over a pair of cheap white tube socks. It was in that moment that the Holy Spirit pointed out to me that my sins left the same stains on my life that the black boots had left on the white socks. I had sinned, and nothing I could do had the power to remove that guilt. However, Jesus, whom I had heard about in church every Sunday, could. As that realization hit me, I fell to my knees and gave my life to Christ. Immediately, the guilt left me. With that action came a new sense of excitement and peace.

I spent that fall of my 9th grade year as a new Christian. All that fall, I had an intense desire to read my Bible, and I spent most days after school laying on my bed reading my Bible. I also pushed my mom to start taking us back to church. We started attending a church thirty minutes away, where some of our friends went.

Unfortunately, I had spent a significant amount of my summer learning to live under compulsion and fear of displeasing God. Those mental habits had started to take root. When I started reading the Bible, much of my reading was in the Old Testament. Occasionally, there are times when God's anger reaches a boiling point. There are times where God takes someone's life because of their disobedience, often for seemingly trivial failures. Unfortunately, I had no one to teach me to put God's actions in context of the events and the rest of the Bible. Also, I didn't fully understand God's character, and that it is defined by love. My Dad would often get very angry at me or my brother when he was working on projects around the house, often over things we did not know were a big deal. There's a saying that your first view of God is a reflection of how you view your parents. Because of these things, I thought God had the same short temper and poorly communicated expectations as my dad.

The church we attended didn't help, either. While Jesus' grace was given lip-service, good behavior was the focus. There was seldom, if ever, teachings of God's love and grace being active in our life. There wasn't a heavy focus on God's goodness and love towards us. To make matters worse, there were some strong cliques in our youth group. There was a tight knit group of friends, whose parents were the Elders in the church (a leadership position), and they were not welcoming of anyone else. I was seeing these same social trends in my school and had hoped for better.

At home, I was struggling heavily with lustful thoughts. When I failed, I felt an incredible amount of guilt. I wasn't learning anywhere to have victory, or that God didn't condemn me, and the guilt piled higher and higher, year after year. I also struggled heavily with being awkward in high school. This led to a lot of loneliness, which exacerbated the lust problem.

As I started college, I did not know how to continue as a Christian. I felt my guilt was a large wall between God and me, and I couldn't overcome it. I had forgotten the very grace that brought me to God in the first place. I spent my college career largely without any regard for my faith.

The summer before my senior year, I was introduced to a business opportunity in the network marketing space. There's a lot that can be said about network marketing. A lot of people have a lot of negative things to say, but that wasn't my experience. I had some negative things happen, but my overall experience has been very positive. It also helped that the team and the company I worked with were fantastic people; people who operated on principle and had good hearts. It was a team made up of very passionate people from all over the country, and most of the leaders were strong Christians. One person in particular challenged me more than anyone else has, simply by sharing his story. The man's name was Jake. There was an incredible transformation that took place for Jake as a result of his journey with these people. When he told stories of what his life was like growing up, it was sometimes hard to believe that the Jake who stood in front of me was the drug dealing, Harley riding Jake that he claims to have been. But the more I got to know him, the more I realized he was telling the truth. Because I wanted what he had, I was drawn to him. His passion and his faith were almost magnetic. As a result of this, I once again decided I wanted to figure all this faith stuff out, but there was one problem. I didn't trust God anymore, and I was afraid of experiencing the prison-like guilt that I knew as a teenager.

I began to build my business on the side of a full-time job. Living in southern West Virginia meant that there was a decent drive to do anything, and I often found myself making 6-hour round trips after work. Thankfully, I had some success in my business. I eventually switched day jobs for a better opportunity in Charleston, the state capital, working for an Oil & Gas company.

The move to the state capital didn't help my problems with loneliness, and I still struggled with guilt. However, the time alone allowed God to deal with my guilt. I began to see that He loved me, despite all of my sinfulness. As my relationship with Him grew, and I began to seek out other Christians as He commands us to do, the loneliness I felt began to wane.

During the spring after I moved, I decided to put a relationship with God first in every area. I had been trying to live out God's principles of victory without having a relationship with Him, and all it did was leave me frustrated. After making that decision, the biggest issue – the issue of loneliness – came front and center. I felt that a big part of what was holding me back in relationships was how much I had let my weight spiral out of control. So, I began trying to diet and exercise, but I kept failing. I was under so much fear and compulsion. Every time I messed up with my diet or missed my exercise, I would beat myself up. Every time I stumbled, this voice in my head kept telling me I should give up and that I would never make. I ended up gaining more weight each time I fell because I would get stuck in this vicious cycle. Eventually, I would eventually pick myself up and try again, but it began to feel hopeless.

During my devotions one evening, I stumbled across a verse in Romans that became my battle cry and set me free. Romans 8:1 (NIV) states: "Therefore, there is now no condemnation for those who are in Christ Jesus." The moment I read this verse, something clicked. Hope welled up in my heart. God was using this verse to tell me that I wasn't condemned for my mistakes.

The first time I messed up after reading this verse and having this revelation is an experience worth retelling. I had slipped up in trying to eat healthy and grabbed a candy bar at work. As I made my way back to my desk, the voice of accusation came back. It whispered into my brain thoughts of how I was a failure. As I sat down at my desk feeling bad for having given into temptation, I saw the yellow sticky note with Romans 8:1 written on it. I immediately spoke out, though quietly so no one else could hear, "There is no condemnation for those who are in Christ." Immediately, both the voice telling me things in the back of my head and the feelings of guilt left. I was floored. I had instantaneously gone from feeling oppressed to feeling liberated. The word says that God's word is a sword, a weapon. In that moment, I had just learned how to use it.

The voice of condemnation continued to try to come back, hoping I would forget to use my weapon … but I was ready. I wrote the verse on sticky notes, and I put it all over my desk at work, on my car dash, and all over my apartment. Every time I failed, and that voice whispered it's condemnation, I met it with my confession of Romans 8:1. Every time without fail, the feelings of guilt and condemnation would instantly disappear. This verse, teamed with my efforts of diet and exercise, enabled me to lose 100 pounds over the next year.

A few months later, I had a second moment where God took the opportunity to root this in my spirit. I was still struggling with loneliness and lust. One summer night, I was dealing with heavy guilt from having given in to lust. That same voice of condemnation was back, but with a different message of condemnation. I knew giving in to lust was very wrong, but I wasn't strong enough to stop it on my own.

It was dark out, and I was out walking by the Kanawha River at Magic Island, a small park on the west side of Charleston. The orange sodium lights dimly lit the winding sidewalk as I wrestled my thoughts. The voice of condemnation had a new front to attack, and it was laying guilt on heavily. It was more aggressive than it had been during the struggle with my weight. The voice went so far to suggest that I shouldn't continue living. At this point in my faith journey, I was still learning how to hear God's Spirit. A part of me that questioned whether this actually was God.

I knew I had failed; was this how God handled guilt? Growing up, I was told it's not respectful to talk back to people in authority. Not knowing if this was God, I didn't want to disrespect Him. But the voice was aggressive, telling me that I deserved to die. I grew increasingly stressed, until I finally snapped. I spoke out strongly into the night air, "God, if you feel I am worthy of death, kill me now. Take me!!"

The silence was deafening as I stood waiting. I was alone in the park, and Charleston is incredibly quiet 10 P.M. during the week. Not even a truck passed on the interstate bridge at the end of the park. The voice had nothing else to say. I waited, prepared to be struck down by God himself. As the silence lingered from my outburst, I began to realize that maybe this wasn't God.

I stood for a minute longer, having stopped my walk when I cried out. Since the voice was no longer speaking, I realized that I wasn't immediately getting struck down, so I began to relax. Slowly, I started walking. As I approached a gnarled crabapple tree, a very different voice began to speak to me in my mind. When this voice spoke, me as I heard each word, there was a peace that filled my soul.

I barely heard the voice at first, but I felt a nudging in my spirit to pick a leaf off of that crab apple tree. In between the webbed veins of the leaf, the flesh of the leaf itself had been mostly eaten to where there was only half of the leaf left. It seemed pathetic to me. The same nudge pushed me to hold the leaf up in front of my face, between me and the lamp post. I did so. The sections of the leaf that hadn't been eaten blocked the light, but the sections that had been eaten allowed the light to shine through. The voice, what the Bible describes as a "still, small voice," spoke a little louder now that it had my attention. In my spirit, I heard the Holy Spirit tell me that, just like this leaf, my flaws allow the light of Jesus to shine through me.

I realized in that moment that God loved me; my inability to be perfect did not matter to Him. I also began to realize that the voice of accusation and guilt wasn't God's voice but was from the enemy.

These experiences were important steps in my journey. Little did I know that the very premises I was learning here would be crucial in the battles that lay ahead. Learning to fight evil thoughts with the power of confessing God's word would be a core part of my battle plan with Samuel. Learning that God's love for me and devotion to me wasn't conditional on my performance was crucial in me understanding that He was always on my side. It helped me realize I could go to Him, and that He wasn't causing the bad things in my life. God isn't looking to cause me harm, he's looking for a tight relationship with me.

My job eventually moved me to Pittsburgh where I went through another period where I struggled with loneliness. At a deeper level, I still struggled with seeing God as a truly loving God. I let heartache and loneliness grow into bitterness, which overtook my life. I made some poor decisions in a relationship with my girlfriend, and she ended up pregnant. This led to even more heartache. We eventually worked everything out, and today we have a healthy co-parenting relationship. In that process, I realized how bitterness was what led me to that point, but I didn't know how to fix it.

As a result, I ended up in another relationship where I found myself making poor decisions. This time also ended in heartache. That relationship ended in May of 2012, when I was 29 years old. Two months later, I met Stephanie. Because of my brokenness, we didn't date immediately. We became close friends and then began dating that winter. I asked her to marry me in August of 2013, and we married in November of that same year. God was fulfilling His promise of setting the lonely in families (Psalms 68:6).

Though I was in a much better spot emotionally, I still didn't fully grasp the goodness of God's character. I struggled with knowing that God wanted good things for me. Growing up, my dad often made the mistake of promising me rewards for doing a task without always fulfilling his promise. If he didn't want to fulfill his promise, he would find some small thing I did wrong and point to that as the reason he couldn't fulfill his promise. My dad is a fantastic dad, and I know he wasn't trying to hurt me. He was often worn out and trying to do the best for his family. His dad was an alcoholic, and my dad overcame many dysfunctions to create a healthy home for us. He didn't realize at the time that he was laying destructive groundwork for his children. As a result, I came into adulthood thinking God did not want me to have the things I wanted unless they lined up perfectly with His will.

I also struggled mightily with the fear that God only tolerated me. My mother grew up in a household fractured by divorce, where she was treated as an unwanted child. She was abused by a neighbor, and she carried with her an immense insecurity of not knowing that she was cherished by God. She didn't know that she was worth fighting for. Since then, she has made incredible strides to overcome her insecurities, but I carried those same thought patterns into adulthood. I didn't know if I was worth fighting for, and I often gave in to others who were in positions of perceived authority, even if they were wrong. I did so, not out of submission, but out of insecurity.

These two beliefs that God didn't want me to have good things in life and the incredible insecurity were flaws in my armor. God would use Samuel's health challenges to pull these out of me and bring me to a place of healing and truth.

HOW TO USE THE FUNKY BOXES (QR CODES)

Aside from the desire as a dad to show off my family, there are certain moments and certain things that just can't be fully captured in text. The images and video bring a reality to our struggles as well as our victories. However, there aren't a lot of good options to share pictures in a book unless you create a picture book. As for videos – well our technology isn't quite there yet.

Thankfully, I found a way to bridge the gap between print and media. Throughout the book, you will see boxes with captions that look like this:

Picture: Izaiah holding Samuel
http://www.rlshawver.com/ftcihp-pic1

To use these, do the following:

1. Access your smartphone camera
2. Point the camera at the QR code
3. Click the link that appears.

From here, you should be able to view the pictures and videos of our journey. If that doesn't work, you will need to download a QR Reader. You can download this from the app store for your device. Then you will open the app and point it at the boxes, like the big one above, and it will allow you to go to the picture or video.

FOR THIS CHILD
I HAVE PRAYED

6 Heart Surgeries, 18 Months

CHAPTER 1

CHOOSING A NAME

"His banner over me is love"
~ Song of Solomon 2:4 NASB

In 2012, I wasn't much of a warrior. I didn't believe in myself enough. I often gave in to the opinions of others and wouldn't trust my own studies. I would have never admitted this to anyone, but it was true. I wasn't ready for the storms that lie ahead.

I spent the first part of the year watching a relationship I was in implode. By May, I ended that relationship definitively and proceeded forward, alone … again, at 29 years old. I had dreamed of being married since I was 5. Yet finding someone who would commit to marriage, or even dating me seriously, eluded me. I realize it's a strange dream for a guy, but I've never claimed to be normal.

After college, while still in my twenties, I moved twice. The first time was to Charleston, WV. For most people, this city is barely big enough to be called a town. To a small-town West Virginia boy, it was the big city. Three years later, my job moved me farther north to Pittsburgh.

The further I moved north, the less southern hospitality I found. Most people I met in Pittsburgh were already part of a tight knit community, which meant there was no room for outsiders like me.

Like anyone, I just wanted a place to belong. After college, I spent a lot of my time trying to prove myself in business. The few relationships I did have never turned into what I hoped they would be. Instead of showing me what I didn't want or helping me get better at relationships, each failed relationship magnified the doubts I had in myself.

This last relationship, I reacted differently. Instead of feeling like a failure, I felt angry at her. I was mad at myself for trusting someone again. Entering the relationship, I had come to the conclusion that I couldn't trust women. I had chosen to trust this girl only because we started as friends. That trust was ill placed. This time, instead of it causing me to lose faith in myself, it caused me to question the ability of finding someone I could trust.

The following month, in June of 2012, I met Stephanie. We were both at a Bible study on a very hot Tuesday evening, coordinated by a church that neither of us attended. I thought her pretty when my eyes spotted her across the open concept living room, standing next to my best friend. I quickly found out she felt the same way. After I saw her the next week at Bible study, we began hanging out. Because the pain from my last relationship was fairly raw and recent, I was hesitant to make any type of commitment to dating anyone. By December, I was ready to commit to dating her. We were married the following November. She was 34 years old when we tied the knot, and I was 30.

Having grown up in a Christian household, I had chosen to become a Christian when I was 15. Although I had struggled in my relationship with my Creator, it was a very real relationship for me. When I met my wife, she was an ordained minister. While most would assume that meant she was pious and only laughed at the cleanest of jokes, one of the reasons I chose to marry her was because she was the least stuffy Christian girl I had met. She had a freedom that appealed to me. She was as willing to dig into the Bible as she was willing to laugh at off-color jokes.

In the months leading up to our marriage, I realized that in order to lead my wife well and to be the husband I wanted to be, I needed to deepen my relationship with God. The month we married, I started a daily habit of waking up early to read my Bible and journal, just to start my day with God. Had I known the benefits, I would have started this habit years earlier.

Given our age, we decided to have children right away. By February, less than 3 months after our wedding, Stephanie was pregnant.

Steph was ecstatic. She came from a large family and wanted 5 kids herself. For her, starting our marriage with a pregnancy was a dream come true. As the initial excitement of the pregnancy calmed, Stephanie turned to the topic of a name for our tiny growing baby.

One night in early March, Stephanie shared her thoughts. She was not quite three months pregnant. "I was thinking," she said, "if we have a girl, I really want to name her. However, if we have a boy, I would like you to name him."

"Ok," I replied. I had not thought yet of naming our child. My mind was thinking more of providing more income.

"If our baby is a girl, I have a name picked out," Stephanie continued.

I smiled and nodded, letting go of my thoughts and focusing on the conversation.

"Rebecca, after my grandmother, and Edith after my mom. Rebecca Edith"

I nodded, "Sure. I like that."

It was settled. Stephanie had been praying for a girl, and I thought nothing more of the conversation. We were fully expecting to have a little girl. Stephanie had been praying for a girl, as I already had a boy with Izaiah. I was excited to honor Stephanie's matriarchs by naming our child after them.

Soon after this conversation, it occurred to me to start praying over this child daily. From that night forward, as we would settle into bed, I would place my hand on Stephanie's belly and pray. I prayed for a lot of different things over the coming months, but one of the earliest and most consistent spiritual urges was to pray for strength. Every single night I prayed for strength for our growing unborn baby. I'm glad the Holy Spirit knew what our baby needed. He knew what lie ahead.

At four and a half months, we went to the OB GYN to determine the sex and to check on the health of the baby. We were surprised to find out that we were not having a girl, but a boy. After the initial astonishment, I realized that I had to come up with a name. Rebecca Edith wasn't the most suitable name for a boy.

I had spent the last 6 months between our wedding and now in awe of how good married life was. I was waking up early every morning to read in Psalms and Proverbs. God had been speaking a lot to me in this period of His love for me and His desire to do good in my life. I had dreamed of having a family since I was a young boy. I was overwhelmed with joy and gratitude because God had given me the desires of my heart. I spent the next few days pondering what to name our son. As I turned it over in my mind, a verse in Revelation occurred to me:

"I will also give that person a white stone
with a new name written on it..."
Rev 2:17 NIV

I also remembered the times in the Bible that God changed people's names. He changed Abram and Sarai to Abraham and Sarah. He changed Jacob to Israel. In the New Testament He changed Saul to Paul. It occurred to me that God had a special name for my son picked out. It gave me great joy to think about giving my son the name God had chosen for him.

Early the next morning, as I finished journaling, I prayed, "God, I would like to honor you. You have been so good to me and have answered my prayers for a wife and a family. I know you have a special name picked out for our son, and if you would be ok with it, I would like to name him that."

I waited a few moments, straining to keep still and hear. I heard nothing, so I continued about the preparations for morning as not to be late to work. Later that evening when I returned home, my wife asked me if I had picked out a name for our boy.

"You know, I was actually praying about that this morning. You know how it says God has a special name for all of us?"

She nodded, putting the finishing touches on dinner.

I continued, "How cool would it be if God allowed us to name our son that name?"

Stephanie didn't seem as thrilled. She wanted a name for our son now.

As the pregnancy progressed, she became less and less thrilled. Every few weeks she asked what I had decided to name our son or if I had heard from God. I continued to wait.

Two weeks and one day before our baby's due date, Stephanie called me at work and told me she was heading to the hospital from work because she was having contractions. She drove herself the few miles to the hospital from her office, and I left work and arrived as fast as I could. I met her in the Emergency Room admittance area, and we checked in together.

As we sat on a padded bench near the entrance, waiting to be called back, another pregnant woman hobbled through the E.R. entrance. She more hobbled than walked. She moved slowly, bent over, face contorted from pain. It was obvious she was in labor. Stephanie took one look at her, turned to me, and said "I'm not in labor."

Since we were already checked in, we went through the process of getting admitted. We stayed at the hospital for a short while before they released her, labelling it Braxton-Hicks's contractions.

The next day, Stephanie had an OB-GYN checkup. We made it home from her checkup around 2 in the afternoon. I had taken off work to go to the appointment with her. As soon as we pulled in the garage, she walked directly to our game room in our basement. She plopped down on a purple pillow-sack and did not move for the rest of the afternoon.

After an hour or two of her not moving and complaining of pain, I suggested she go to the hospital. She refused.

After a few hours more of trying to do all I could to comfort her, I had a realization; She didn't want to go back to the hospital because was embarrassed from what had happened the day before. She wanted to wait until she was sure she was in labor before heading back. I, on the other hand, was very sure that this was the moment.

It took me 5 hours to convince her that she was actually in labor this time. During that time, Izaiah's mom dropped Izaiah off at our house. I spent my time that evening helping him adjust to our house and to trying to convince Stephanie that it was a good decision to go to the hospital.

Around 9 PM, Stephanie finally gave in to my pushing. She called her sister Zoi, who came over to watch Izaiah. I grabbed our bags and Stephanie waddled to the car. When we finally were able to leave, it was close to 10.

We arrived at the hospital at 10:45 PM, taking the route we knew (even though it was nowhere near the shortest or the fastest). When we finally arrived at the ER, Stephanie was far enough in her birth process that she almost missed the window for an epidural.

In the midst of all the chaos, it wasn't lost on me that I still had not heard from God on a name for my son. During a lull in the pain and contractions, Stephanie asked sternly, "Do you have a name yet?"

I reassured her, "I don't, but if I don't hear from God, I will choose a name."

She continued, already upset from the pain, "I just don't want to have an 'Unnamed baby Shawver' sign hanging over his crib for a couple of days."

I managed to reassure her that this would not be the case, just before we were interrupted by a nurse.

As the nurse tended to Stephanie, I weighed out the options in my mind. "How long should I wait?" In the entirety of my life up until that moment, I would have felt incredibly anxious about waiting on

God. Instead, I felt perfectly calm. I had prayed to God, and I knew if He did not deliver a name to me, He had a good reason. If God didn't share the name He had chosen for my son, I would choose one.

I knew that I really liked the name David because he was my favorite historical figure from the Bible. He was a fierce warrior and a man who had stood on God's promise while being chased for years through the wilderness.

I also liked Ronald. While I go by my initials, it is both my dad's and my own first name. Ronald means "Wise Ruler." Given its meaning, I've sometimes been disappointed to keep my name hidden all my life. "My son could be Ronald the third," I thought. I could continue the tradition of my dad and myself, and we could embrace the name and the meaning.

My musings were interrupted with the need to take care of the next step in the birthing process. I didn't get another moment that night to think about the name. Stephanie had a quick labor, and every moment after was a bustle of activity in our delivery room.

At 2:12 in the morning, less than four hours after we were admitted, our baby boy was born. As I reached to take him in my arms the first time, my beautiful wife looked at me and asked flippantly, "Do you have a name for him yet?"

I knew it was time to decide. As I took him in my arms, I felt an overwhelming feeling of joy. The joy was accompanied by a warm fire in my soul, and I felt, rather than heard, the name Samuel.

I was shocked. Samuel had never been a consideration.

I silently prayed, "God, are you sure? I was really warming towards Ronald or David." As I prayed in my head, the thought of a name other than Samuel caused the joy to flee my soul, leaving an emptiness in its wake. I had never experienced such intense feelings before.

As I pondered the name Samuel, the joy and fire flooded my soul again.

I deliberated in my head for a moment more. "God, the first-born son that my mentor lost was named Samuel. Are you sure?" Jake was a long-time hero of mine. He was currently my business mentor, and his first son was still born. This was during an incredibly hard transition period for Jake and his wife Jackie. He was in the first year of business, all while working a full-time job and focusing on much needed and very intense personal growth. They were on the verge of foreclosure with their first home, their truck had been repossessed, and he ended up getting fired from his job. Jake and Jackie had often spoke emotionally of the son they had lost. I did not want to dishonor their family, and I surely didn't want to hurt the man who had been mentoring me.

As I asked God again about choosing some other name than Samuel, the overwhelming joy was once again gone, as if turned off by a switch. In its place came confusion and emptiness.

God was persistent. It was settled. I turned to my wife and offered her my decision, "Samuel. We'll call him Samuel. Samuel Aaron Shawver. Aaron to honor my best friend."

Aaron had been my closest friend for many years. He had been there for me through the best and worst of times. He was a loyal and supportive friend.

To my surprise, Stephanie immediately took to the name. "I love it," she grinned.

She gushed with joy over her newborn son. I admired him and my beautiful wife. As we held him in our arms, we noticed our Samuel wheezing gently with each breath. I thought it cute. The room had emptied from the crowd of doctors and nurses. It was just the three of us.

Picture: Just after birth
http://www.rlshawver.com/ftcihp-pic5

Occasionally a nurse would enter to take check Samuel's and Stephanie's vitals. On one such entrance, one of the nurses told Stephanie that the wheezing was a sign he had fluid on his lungs. Stephanie relayed the information to me after the nurse left. Even with that information, I thought nothing of it. I assumed it was normal for a newborn. It must have been, as they had not taken him from our room. I promptly fell asleep on the couch in the room, leaving my wife to laugh at my ability to fall asleep anywhere. Sometime during the night, the nurses took Samuel up to the NICU.

The next morning, Stephanie and I went up to visit Samuel. A doctor who was working in the NICU updated us on Samuel. Stephanie caught all the details, as I was too busy keeping track of my oldest son, who was with us for the weekend, and my parents. My parents had joined us that morning, after sleeping at our house the night before. They had missed his birth by less than an hour in the long trek to Pittsburgh after we called them to tell them we were going to the hospital. This was now their opportunity to gush over their new grandson. We observed him through the protective glass, each of us waiting our turn to go in and see him. As we waited outside the glass, we could see his heart monitor.

My mom pointed out Samuel's heartbeat to me. It was beating at 260 beats a minute. When I asked Stephanie about his heartbeat, she told me what the doctor had told her. He called the condition SVT, or Super-Ventricular Tachycardia. I caught the information, but I was too distracted to fully comprehend. My oldest son, Izaiah, was just shy of 4 years old. He was climbing and hanging off everything, and I was trying to keep him from hurting himself or breaking something. My parents were not familiar with the big city, and they were now ready to go back to my house and rest. No doctors were calling for emergency surgery for Samuel, so I assumed that all was well.

Later that day, the doctors ran a battery of tests, including an echocardiogram to check the function of his heart. They discovered that Samuel's mitral valve, the internal valve on the left side of his heart, wasn't closing correctly. When the valve was supposed to be closed to allow blood to flow forward, it was only closing halfway, and a lot of blood was flowing backwards. They called it severe mitral valve regurgitation.

On top of that, Samuel also was dealing with jaundice. He had to spend his first few days under purple lights in an incubator. He looked like a rock star with the large eye covering. The cover looked like sunglasses, and the violet light mimicked stage lighting. I joked with Stephanie that he was our little rock star, attempting to keep the mood light.

We were concerned, but we didn't take the doctor's prognosis as anything ominous. We had prayed over him daily that he would be a strong healthy baby and we expected he would be fine. In fact, strength was one of the things that God prompted us to pray over him the most. We didn't realize when we were praying over him in Stephanie's womb that God was preparing Samuel for the storms that lie ahead.

Even though Samuel ended up spending a full week in the hospital, we were home before his due date. The doctors sent us home with some medication to be administered orally, which would keep his heart in a regular rhythm. Despite the medical problems, Stephanie and I were joyous and calm. I knew our prayers were being answered and we both glowed with the excitement of our baby. I assumed the medical issues were a non-issue. I was right about our prayers being answered, but I was very wrong about this being a non-issue.

CHAPTER 2

HE'S BLUE!

"I will call upon Your Name and keep my eyes
above the waves...." ~ Hillsong United

"He's blue!" Stephanie screamed from the living room. "Babe!
Samuel's blue."

I bolted into the living room.

—◊—

Stephanie had taken Samuel to his pediatrician that morning. I
stayed home and slept.

Samuel was 2-1/2 months old. He wasn't eating properly and
was acting fussier than normal. He had been for the past two days.
Stephanie picked up on it immediately and had been fretting all night.
As soon as she woke that morning, she attempted to feed him again.
When he still wouldn't eat, she took him to his pediatrician.

She woke me before she left. I tried to tell her he would be fine.
She didn't listen, and I fell back to sleep.

It was Saturday, the last in November. It had snowed less than an
inch of wet snow overnight, and fog had covered the valleys between
the rolling hills that are so common around Pittsburgh.

I thought my wife was being overly concerned. I was convinced it was "first-time mom instincts" driving her to see issues that weren't really there. After all, I had prayed to God that Samuel's heart issues would be healed. I was confident that Samuel didn't need any extra attention. God was handling it. Right?

Samuel had spent his first week of life at West Penn hospital. West Penn is on the eastern side of Pittsburgh between two sections of town called Lawrenceville and East Liberty. It is less than a mile from Children's Hospital of Pittsburgh. The two are separated by long lines of row houses of all different colors, many in need of a little extra care.

Between the SVT (racing heart) and the bad heart valve, the hospital staff worked diligently to keep his heart beating steady and pumping well. They spent the week adjusting Samuel's dosage of heart regulation medications to get his heart beating normally.

The room at West Penn where Stephanie and Samuel stayed reminded me of a New York City apartment. The hallways were surprisingly dark for a hospital. I only came in the evenings, after I had finished work. I'm guessing they dimmed the hallway lights at night, which made the hospital seem even more like an old apartment complex. The room was small and yellow, with little unused area to maneuver. The crib barely fit between the door frame and the wall. The door had to be closed to allow entrance to an incredibly small bathroom that could have had a previous life on an airplane. There was a small TV near the only window, which was dingy with age. The window overlooked a circular park with the only street parking nearby. The parking garage for the hospital was incredibly expensive, so I always parked on that circle, and Stephanie could always see my car when I arrived.

Given the state of the room and the circumstances, I felt as if my wife and son were living in an entirely different city. It was a strange feeling. I had expected to take the entire week off work to spend time bonding with Samuel. Since he was spending the week in the hospital and the room was so small, I returned to work. By the end of the week, I felt incredibly disconnected from my wife and brand-new son. To compound matters, Stephanie was processing the ramifications of her new son and his medical conditions internally, and my work kept me very busy. I had hoped to bond. Instead, I felt hundreds of miles away. It made my first week of being Samuel's father very lonely.

When Samuel was close to 6 weeks old, we had to take him back down to the hospital. This time, he was sent to Children's Hospital of Pittsburgh, instead of West Penn. He wasn't eating properly, and Stephanie was starting to get concerned. All parents deal with their child not eating from time to time. Given most babies aren't talking at that age, they aren't the most forthcoming in telling a parent what is bothering them. Samuel was no exception, and it was often difficult to tell if he was not eating because of bad gas or because of something more sinister.

When Stephanie arrived at Children's hospital, the nurses ran the standard tests at check-in, checking his blood pressure, height, weight, and pulse. His heart was beating at over 200 beats per minute. He was in SVT.

The hospital kept Samuel a full week, and Stephanie never left his side. Once again, they worked to keep his heart rate under control with proper medication. This week was incredibly stressful for me. I couldn't stand not being able to come home every night to my wife and son, but I also couldn't afford to take time off from work. Stephanie was so incredibly focused on his medical care and being attentive to him that there was little room for me. I did not want to have to experience that level of loneliness again.

When Stephanie came home from the pediatrician that morning, she insisted there was still something wrong. The doctor had told her she should go ahead and take him to the hospital. I was just starting to wake when she came in the house. Stephanie left Samuel in his car seat in the living room floor beside the couch and came to talk with me.

"I think I should take him to the hospital," she told me.

Still groggy, I dismissed her concerns. I'm not sure if she failed to mention that the doctor thought it was a good idea, or I missed it in my morning sleepiness. Either way, I'll take the blame. "Babe, I'm sure he's going to be fine," I tried to reassure her.

She said nothing more. I went back to my morning reading and Stephanie went back to the living room. I assumed he was being finnicky with his eating because of his age. In the back of my mind, I did not want to lose more time away from my wife unless it was necessary. The stays at the hospital were so exhausting to me, given the newness of our marriage. We had just celebrated our first wedding anniversary a few days prior.

As I sat in bed reading my Bible, Stephanie startled me with loud shouts. "Samuel's blue!"

I rushed into the living room. Samuel's face was a light shade of blue, and his lips a much darker shade of blue.

I called 911 while Stephanie gathered Samuel and his diaper bag.

I quickly relayed the situation to the dispatcher and gave her our address. After we made it through the important details, I asked the dispatcher how long it would take for the ambulance to arrive. I had been on my feet, pacing.

As I asked the question, I walked out the front door, hoping to pace on the porch to expend my nervous energy. Our living room was too small, and I was too tense. The black wrought iron fencing that lined our porch was a stark contrast to the mist and the spots of snow on the still-green grass.

"We have someone in the area," the dispatcher replied. "They should be there in about 15 minutes."

"Fifteen minutes?" I queried, holding my voice steady but shocked at the time it would take for them to arrive. We lived very close to the city, in the well populated suburbs of Pittsburgh.

"Yes," she replied.

I did a quick mental calculation. It was less than a 5-minute drive to the local hospital.

"Hold on," I said, covering the microphone with the palm of my hand. I stuck my head in the door to the house and asked Stephanie, "Should we just take him?"

We conferred for a moment on the details, my hand still over the phone to shield the dispatcher from our conversation. The dusting of snow and icy spots on the road would not be a problem if we were cautious. It was early December.

"Sure," Stephanie said, without much prompting.

"We can get there before the ambulance gets here," I replied, echoing her thoughts. I almost forgot I was still on the phone with 911.

Stephanie nodded her head in agreement as it dawned on me that I should answer the dispatcher. Our conversation had been quick, and the woman on the other end was still filling me in on details.

Pulling my hand off the microphone, I interrupted her calmly, "We'll just take him."

"So, we have all the details, we will have someone on the way," the dispatcher continued, not realizing what I had said.

"We changed our mind," I reiterated. "We are going to take him. We can be there before an ambulance can get to our house."

She took a moment to comprehend what I was saying. "You are going to take him?" she asked, a hint of surprise in her tone.

It took a moment or two more to get the orders for an ambulance canceled, but I had made up my mind. I would typically have been concerned with disappointing or burdening someone, but I felt the urgency outweighed my concerns for the dispatcher's feelings.

Hanging up the phone, I gathered my keys and threw on my coat. I walked out the door and Stephanie followed close behind, holding Samuel close to her. He was swaddled as they had taught us in our baby class, then wrapped again with his white fuzzy blanket. Stephanie hopped into the front seat of my steal-blue four door sedan, holding Samuel in her lap.

"You don't want to do the car seat?" I queried without emotion.

"No, he'll be fine."

I nodded. She would be able to better handle him in case he needed immediate medical attention. We wouldn't get above the 35-mph necessary to engage the airbags. There were three stop lights between us and the hospital and I really wanted to blow through each of them. The first crossed 5 lanes of traffic on McKnight Road, and I didn't think it wise.

We sat at the light, anxiously awaiting its turn to green. The only words we spoke were my questions for status update and Stephanie's answers; my mind was hyper-focused on the task at hand – getting my small family to the hospital as quickly and safely as possible.

When the light turned green, we crossed all five lanes and made our way onto the winding road past Stephanie's favorite restaurant and the tiny campus for LaRoche college.

Three cars were sitting at the second light as we approached. I stopped. Waiting for it to change, I considered driving around them on the right and driving through the intersection. After a quick glance, I noticed there wasn't the room to do so safely. We sat again in silence waiting on the second light. Mercifully, it changed shortly after we stopped.

We managed to catch a red light at the third intersection as well, but this time I was able to go around the stack of cars in the gravel beside the road. I turned right into the hospital, ignoring the thoughts that I might be angering some random person by my impatience. I sped down the length of road beside the hospital to the Emergency Room entrance. As I pulled into the parking lot, I wasn't paying attention and mistakenly pulled into the ambulance entrance, as opposed to the admissions entrance. Two EMTs stood beside the door, chatting after a call. One of them spoke up as Stephanie hopped out with Samuel, "You guys are supposed to use the Admittance entrance."

I had already hopped out to help Stephanie grab her stuff. I paused, looking around to see where the entrance was. As I did so, he must have realized the situation; reading the fear on my wife's face and noticing her clutching her baby, he waved her on. "Don't worry about it, just come on inside," he said.

I nodded and went straight to Stephanie, making sure she had what she needed. As she quickly walked into the door, clutching Samuel to her chest, I hopped back into the car and whipped it into the first spot I could find.

I entered through the main Emergency entrance. Just past the doors, a guard sat behind a small brown table, next to a walk-through metal detector. As I approached, he asked to see my book bag, which I carried everywhere. He took it from me and began to slowly unzip and dig through each pocket.

I walked through the metal detector, depositing my keys on one side, and picking them up on the other. After I went through, I turned to the security guard to grab my bag. He had only searched the first pocket and seemed intent on searching every single compartment. I stood watching, my body tense - anxious to get to my family. As he slowly unzipped the second side pocket, having not even touched the main compartment, I grunted in exasperation.

"Fine, bring it to me," I blurted. Even though this bag went everywhere with me, I didn't care.

The look on his face spoke volumes of annoyance and surprise, but I wasn't sticking around to hear his protests. I waited only long enough to make sure he heard me, and then I bolted towards the doorway to the trauma rooms. I entered the first set of double doors at admissions, rapidly informing the ladies behind the counter, "My son's already back there." One of them buzzed me in, after a momentary pause of confusion, and I went to the main nursing station and asked where they put Samuel. They directed me to his room.

He lay on an adult bed that had the sides pulled up. They already had an oxygen mask on him, the smallest adult size they could find. It engulfed his entire 2-1/2-month-old face. The normally tiny hospital bed seemed the size of a kitchen table compared to my tiny baby boy. The room appeared incredibly white that morning. Samuel was already pale, and the white walls and light oak laminated cabinets added to the aura. The TV, blood pressure cuff, and pastel teal curtain were the only punctuation in a sea of light.

Eventually the security guard brought my backpack to me. I brushed off his annoyance with a curt thank you. I was focused on my son, annoyed at the delay his search caused. I was frustrated at what I perceived to be his lack of perspective. He's working in a hospital, slowing people from entering an Emergency Room.

The doctors soon told us that Samuel had a lot of fluid on his lungs. They decided the best course of action was to take him to Children's Hospital. They sent for a Life-Flight team to take Samuel on the 30-minute drive to Children's Hospital, which is in an older section of the city of Pittsburgh called Lawrenceville. We were gathering as much information as we could process. At first, we didn't think to ask why Samuel couldn't be taken to Children's hospital in a normal ambulance.

Within a few minutes of our arrival, Stephanie's mom showed up. Stephanie and I stood next to Samuel, doing anything we could to reassure and comfort our tiny baby. She would step away occasionally to talk with a nurse and ask questions, but I refused to step away from him. I leaned over his bed, keeping my hand on his arm, or gently stroking his blonde hair. I had been praying and declaring God's healing over Samuel since I found out he had SVT. My mind dug up any thought that could be of assistance. A passage in Psalms (Psalms 22:3) sprang to my mind, "The Lord inhabits the praises of His people." I was clinging to the things I had read, the promises that God is our healer. I knew He could. I felt we just needed His presence.

With my face close to his and my hands caressing his head, I sang. I was determined to sing God's praises over my two and half month-old son. I sang the only worship song that sprang to my mind. It was a song by Hillsong United, a worship band from a church out of Australia. I don't listen to much music on the radio, but it was seemingly everywhere.

I sang softly, over and over, as I stood bent over his bed.

"Spirit lead me where my trust is without borders;
Let me walk upon the waters
Wherever you would call me.
Take me deeper than my feet could ever wander.
And my faith will be made stronger
In the presence of my Savior."

In hindsight, I chuckle at singing a song asking God to draw me deeper in the waters. I also chuckle that this was one of the few worship songs I knew and liked well enough to sing. I sang, and I stood beside his bed. I eventually began playing the music on my phone and sang with it. I only knew five lines, and I needed more in the long wait. I was not going to leave my son's side.

After twenty minutes of waiting, we asked how long it would take for the helicopter to arrive. The nurse replied, "The weather is too bad for the life flight team to fly today."

Stephanie and I were caught off guard, puzzled at how mist and a little bit of snow could make the weather too bad to fly.

"They are dispatching a team to drive. They are coming from the South Hills," she finished.

The South Hills is on the other side of Pittsburgh. Due to the poor road grid, the ambulance driver would have to drive through multiple neighborhoods, through downtown, and up through the roads of the North Hills to get to us. Although it was a Saturday and traffic shouldn't be quite as bad as rush hour, it was also three weeks before Christmas. One of the nurses told us it would take forty-five minutes. Every minute seemed to pass with slow diligence, as if it couldn't be rushed from the tasks at hand.

Unlike other visits, we were never left alone in the room. I assume this was due to the serious nature of Samuel's immediate condition.

"Why can't an ambulance team drive him to Children's?" Stephanie eventually asked one of the nurses or doctors who had rotated into the room, both of us struggling to keep all the emotion and the activity from overwhelming us.

"Life-Flight teams have Registered Nurses," the nurse or doctor informed us, "not just EMTs, and they are able to better handle emergency situations." Satisfied with her answer, we turned back to Samuel, and to waiting.

The Life Flight team finally showed up after an hour and fifteen minutes from the time of dispatch. Their dark blue uniforms contrasted sharply with the white of Samuel's room. I spoke briefly with them and encouraged them to take care of my wife and son.

Stephanie asked if I wanted to ride in the ambulance with Samuel to Children's. I deferred to her, and she chose to go. I volunteered to go home and pack her a bag and take care of our dog.

Soon after Samuel arrived at UPMC Children's Hospital of Pittsburgh, the doctors admitted him. We spent the next few days waiting on the doctors to decide what a game plan going forward.

The medical staff finally determined the best course of action was open heart surgery. I had been believing that God was taking care of Samuel, and that he would be ok. I knew I needed to talk to my mentor. Jake had been coaching me through my network marketing business for about a year. I had dreamed of him being my mentor for most of my time in business. He had become a huge success in his business, his family, and his faith – all things that I valued. I had hoped to earn that mentorship through the success of my business, but instead I had earned it more by a series of events outside of my control.

Jake had built a team of over a thousand active business owners, and my business was a small part of his team. I tried to be extremely mindful of how I used his time, partially out of respect and partially due to a poor self-image. I kept my messages to him short, typically in a text message or through our business communications platform. I updated him weekly on my business activity and growth, when I was working with a new partner, or when I had questions. This time was no different except for the context. I shot him a text before leaving for the hospital.

I was driving on a back road that cut through a tiny old town between two hill tops called Millvale when he texted back. The road was spotted with businesses and residential areas. It wound gently beside a small stream that cut through the hilltops and lead to one of Pittsburgh's major rivers. The glow of the sodium lights that lined the road painted everything orange, punctuated by neon lights of the small mom and pop shops and restaurants. At one of the stop lights, I checked his message and responded. I had been keeping him aware of the underlying problems, and we were both hoping for a less intrusive outcome.

He responded in his typical boldness, with which I was very familiar.

"Check out Psalm 91, and I want you to grab a couple of books. Let me get back to you on the names," he replied. Before I arrived at the hospital, he texted again, "I want you to get these: 'The Wonderful Name of Jesus' by Kenyon, 'Redeemed (from Poverty, Sickness, and Spiritual Death)' by Kenneth Hagin, and 'The Power of a Praying Parent' by Stormie O'Martian." Jake was a bold guy, not because he didn't care, but because he did. I knew he was taking on a lot by mentoring me in business, and now in my journey for the healing of my son.

I made it to the hospital to visit Stephanie and Samuel that evening. The next morning, I ordered the books while at work.

When they arrived, I started reading "The Wonderful Name of Jesus" with every moment I had to spare. I worked through it quickly over the next few days. After I finished, I jumped immediately into "Redeemed." Most of the information was not new to me, but it was compact and intense. Also, I had never had the opportunity to really put these principles in practice. These premises and promises of God's word were my first steps forward.

CHAPTER 3

A SMALL STITCH

"I HAVE SOME CONCERNS."
~ BAYMAX FROM "BIG HERO 6"

I got started in business with Jake's team when I was 21 years old. For the next ten years, I studied his attitude and his mindset about business and life. I looked up to Jake. He had overcome many struggles in his life that would cripple most people.

Jake had grown up in an alcoholic household. Because of that, he grew up knowing how to fight. His background and tenacity led him early on to a successful trade in illicit substances. After a few life-altering events at age 19, he decided that joining the Marine Corp would be a better path to pursue. It was there that he met his wife, who grew up in a tiny desert town in southern California that was attached to the largest Marine Corps base in the world. They eventually married and moved to North Carolina, where Jake's softball coach introduced him to a group of entrepreneurs who were expanding a business. Jake's successes in life to that point had only taught him only how to fight physically to win. His new entrepreneurial associates taught him how to mold that fighting spirit into something more positive and productive. He went on to develop a very large and influential business, of which my team was a very small part.

While Jake's primary purpose was to coach people to success in business; he also taught people to succeed in all areas of their life, just as Jake's coaches had taught him. A huge part of how Jake taught me to live a successful life was by showing me how to reframe my relationship with God.

In the churches where I was raised, God was framed as a God of judgement, a God who watched us closely to catch us in sin. We were cattle, and He was steering us towards a sinless life, herding us along with the whip of guilt and the rod of fear. The pastors I grew up listening to taught, through their words and actions, that the ultimate goal was to live a sinless a life. While this framework didn't line up with what I had read in the Bible, it was difficult as a youth to know how to take a stand and how to trust my own interpretations. These pastors and church leaders were experts, right? I knew something was wrong, but I couldn't articulate what that was.

Jake and his wife Jackie, as well as the other leaders they worked with in business, had a very different view of God. At first, all I saw was their success in business, but it didn't take long to see that they had a strong relationship with God. The more I studied these businessmen and women, the more I realized that their view of God was vastly different from the people in the churches of my youth.

When I heard Jake speak or spent time around him, his enthusiasm about his business was surpassed by his enthusiasm for his God. His understanding of God echoed what I had read throughout the Bible. His passion and experience were the missing ingredients in what I was taught as a youth. He exemplified an intimate relationship with God. I had heard preaches talk of that intimacy, of that but never saw any fruit of it. Jake spoke of a God who still operated in the miraculous – in healing, in provision, where I had only known a God defined by judgement. He spoke of a good God who loves in action, and not only in words. Jake's life experiences and how he handled them inspired me to seek God. At that moment, as I fought for Samuel's life, I was honored to have his words directing my steps.

The books that Jake had suggested for me to read directed me on how to stand against the fears that threatened to overwhelm me. In that first month after we found out that Samuel was going to have surgery, I was crushed. If I were a boat, and life was an ocean, the fear was a category 5 hurricane. It engulfed my life and everything around me in tumult and darkness.

The fear waged war against my mind on two separate fronts.

The first front was the residual feeling of fear, that constant feeling that something bad is going to happen or is happening. It clung to me like a thick grease. Thankfully, I knew how to fight this battle. I knew this game.

Over the years, I've discovered my feelings are often the fruit of what I am consistently thinking. What I let my mind constantly dwell on became my expectations, and those expectations steered my emotions. The more I directed my thoughts by confessing God's promises, instead of confessing what I feared, the more that the residual crushing feeling of fear faded. The leaders in Jake's business were the ones responsible for teaching me how to deal with my emotions, especially how to deal with fear.

Faced with the prospect of open-heart surgery for my 2-month-old son, I was devastated. I had expected Samuel to be healed completely, for us to be able to live like normal parents.

Heart surgery was a surprise. So many questions plagued my mind. What would his life be like after surgery? Would he make it through the surgery? Why was God allowing this to happen?

To continue the boat analogy, waves of analysis, question, and worry threatened to swallow my ship whole.

In those rough seas, my confession became my anchor.

My first major confession was a simplification of a verse I had stumbled upon in Psalm 112 about those who fear (honor) God:

Ps 112:2 NIV "Their children will be mighty in the land; the generation of the upright will be blessed."

I knew that for Samuel to be mighty in the land, he would have to grow to an age where he could be mighty. Babies, by default, aren't mighty. Someone could say they were mighty for a baby, but I don't see God as a God who tries to get by on technicalities. If God is saying my son would be mighty, I knew Samuel would have to grow to be a man to become mighty.

The other reason why I knew this verse applied to me was because of my righteousness. I know how arrogant that sounds, so please let me clarify. I was not righteous because of my actions. I was made righteous because of my faith in God and His son Jesus. Nothing more. My righteousness was actually a gift, a byproduct of what Jesus did for me (see Romans 8:5). I didn't earn that righteousness; it was freely given. If this is foreign to you, check out the last chapter – "How to have a relationship with God."

So, my paraphrase of Psalms 112:2 became my go to confession. Every night, I made my declaration of God's word out loud as I tucked

Samuel in his hospital bed or his crib at home. "Samuel will live long in the land and grow strong in the land."

The second manifestation of fear came in the form of images and visions. Every time my mind slowed down, the visions came. The visions attempted to overwhelm me and often left me visibly shaken. They would pop suddenly and vividly into my head, flying into my mind like pop-up ads in a cheap app on a smartphone.

In one such vision, Stephanie and I were at a funeral standing in front of a tiny baby casket. Stephanie was wearing a black dress, her head covered with a black veil. I stood, holding my sobbing wife, trying to make sense of our baby's death. Every dark vision always revolved around Samuel's death.

Those visions came over me intensely for those first few months, but the lessons I had learned in my twenties trained me exactly how to handle this. I knew it was a demonic force that was trying to get me to accept this as our future.

These demonic forces were trying to wreck my faith that God would heal my son. What you see in your mind is the picture of your faith. Satan and his demons knew if they could firmly place that image in my head - the death of my son – they would have successfully destroyed my faith. They would have won, and my prayers would be ineffective.

I met each vision head-on with my confession of God's word. Sometimes, there were parts of the Bible that I studied well enough to recognize a promise from God that directly conflicted with what this vision was showing me. Other times, I simply went back to that same expectation, "Samuel will live long in the land and grow strong in the land." I always made my confessions out loud. If I was able, I would declare them loudly. If Samuel was sleeping, or if there were others present who wouldn't understand, I whispered them. The stronger the visions were, the angrier I became. I knew Satan had corrupted Samuel's heart and health, and he was trying to keep his death-grip on Samuel's health.

For every piece of bad news or every fear or evil image, my confession was my weapon. God's word was my sidearm – every time fear reared its wicked head, in any form, I shot it squarely in the face – "Samuel will live long in the land and grow strong in the land."

When Stephanie arrived at the hospital the next morning, after Samuel had been rushed there the day before, she spoke with the Head of the Fellowship program, Dr. Bresnan. He and his team were the ones who chose to do the surgery. Stephanie relayed the information to me on the phone while I was at work. Unfortunately, I was not granted any extra time off above what was normally allotted with sick time and vacation, and I was almost out of vacation time for the year, so I had to take the phone call at my desk in front of my computer. I stewed on the information all day, dealing with the main question, why didn't God heal Samuel? As I left work that evening, I sent a text to Jake, telling him when Samuel was scheduled for surgery. We chatted briefly over text, while he encouraged me with more verses of God's protection to declare, to believe, and on which I could stand.

Stephanie informed me that the doctors would make their rounds the next morning and would be able to answer any questions I had, so I took off from work the next morning. I made it to the hospital by 7 AM, so I could catch the doctors as they made their rounds. Dr.

Arora was the lead doctor on Samuel's case. He entered the room with two young doctors who working on their fellowship program.

I may have met Dr. Arora in some of Samuel's prior appointments, but I don't remember meeting him before that morning. Since Stephanie worked part time, she had taken Samuel to all of his appointments. I had only been at a few.

Dr. Arora pulled up a chair and sat across from us in the hospital room to set us at ease. He was a short man of Indian descent. He was somewhere between ten and twenty years my senior, but he had a youthful face and a quick smile that made it hard to guess his age. He also had a youthful exuberance, as well as an interest in people and in taking on new challenges. This warmth in his personality hid the fierce way in which he attacked the medical problems concerning his patients. He spoke quickly that morning, which I later realized was just his nature. After quick introductions of himself and the fellows shadowing him, he got straight to the point.

"So, we are going to do open heart surgery on Samuel on Friday. We are going to open him up, and then we will put a small stitch in Samuel's mitral valve," he told us.

My engineering mind ran wild with questions, "Really?" I queried. This didn't seem to make sense. Stitching closed, or partially closed, a valve that's supposed to open and close seemed like it would cause more problems.

"Yes," he replied. "The surgeon will go in and put a small stitch between two of the leaflets," unfazed by my hesitancy.

"What about a replacement heart valve?" I asked.

"No, he is much too small for that right now," Dr. Arora replied patiently.

"Won't this make things worse?" I asked, my fear continuing to rise.

He started to reply, but I interrupted, "Wouldn't it make it harder in the opposite direction? Instead of him now having too much blood coming back, wouldn't it cause the blood to not flow properly?" As much as I was trying to grasp what was going on, I also was still struggling with the question of why. In all reality, I still had not let go of my expectation that Samuel would not need open heart surgery.

"No, it actually doesn't work that way," he replied, his voice taking a calming tone, a tone he had no doubt used on thousands of worried parents before today. "This will actually allow the valve to open and close better."

Somewhat satisfied with his answer, but still feeling anxious, I continued. "What happens when he gets older?"

Dr. Arora, still unphased, tilted his head slightly to the right, "Well, when stenosis happens, we will deal with that surgery later. This is just meant to get him a couple of months till he gets bigger."

This left me more shocked, but it ended my questioning. I opened my mouth to make another query, but I could think of nothing else to ask.

Stephanie placed her hand on my arm as I opened my mouth. "It's ok, babe," she whispered. She had had time to process the situation the night before.

As I sat thinking of what this meant, I just didn't feel right. This wasn't what I had been praying for or expecting. It seemed God was taking us down a different path.

Reluctantly, I was realizing that we were going to have to wait on God's deliverance.

The day before the surgery, Samuel's surgeon, Dr. Morell, came in to speak with us. Dr. Victor Morell is in many ways the opposite of Dr. Arora. He is 6'3", with curly shorter hair lightened to the chestnut brown of an avid surfer. His bedside manner also echoed that of a seasoned surfer. His smile and ease were a stark contrast to the ever-present tension one would expect in a heart surgery wing of a children's hospital. I'm sure his calm demeanor and broad smile worked well at calming fearful parents and patients alike. Nothing seemed to faze him. We met many people whose children were operated on by Dr. Morell, many with tales of seemingly impossible surgical feats; pediatric heart surgery was his specialty.

During one of Samuel's later operations, we met one parent who told us of how their child was born with two chambers in their child's heart, instead of the usual four. As we both sat waiting in the waiting room for our children to exit surgery, the surgeons a few rooms away were repairing, almost creating, a heart that had not been fully formed. The feats these Doctors were performing were nothing short of miraculous.

Dr. Morell would be going inside Samuel's stilled heart, which wasn't much bigger than a walnut, and placing a stitch on the edge of the leaflets of the valve.

His description to us sounded much less complicated. "We are going to put him under, and then I am going to put a small stitch in his valve. That's it," he said in his slight accent, which sounded South

American, gesturing that he would be done by moving both hands facing out.

At this point, we only nodded. The shock of the turn of events left us in a haze. My thoughts were swirling, a winter wind kicking up the snow. I knew a blizzard was approaching, but there was nothing I could do to stop it.

The next morning brought with it early sunlight streaming into Samuel's Seventh Floor room. Soon after, a nurse came to take Samuel to prep him for surgery. The nurse in charge of transporting him moved his entire bed into the hallway but did not invite us to go with her. She directed us to the 4th floor waiting area through the main elevators. Samuel was the first patient on the schedule for the day, and they took him at 6 A.M. We blearily but quickly made our way to the elevator and down from the 7th floor. Since the 4th floor houses both the cardiac ICU (CICU) and the operating rooms, there was very little in the way of open hallways. A square section of purple walls immediately surrounded the elevators, an attempt to break up the monotony of hospital white floors and walls and lights.

To the south as you enter the 4th floor was a set of oak double doors you only see in hospitals or old dormitories. To the right was a t-intersection. Just past the intersection to the left were the public restrooms for the floor and a water fountain. We would soon find that the hallway to the right of the t-intersection was where the prep rooms and the OR were situated, hidden behind another set of double oak doors. To the left of the t-intersection was a relatively short, in hospital terms, hallway. To the left of that hallway were the waiting rooms for the OR, and the door at the end of the hallway led to the waiting rooms for the CICU.

The waiting room had a glass door, and the walls were painted a muted red while the floor was covered with beige carpets. The room was laid out in an elongated fashion, left to right as you entered. To the right, the walls were lined with chairs. A TV hung in the corner, next to two very large full-length windows looking off towards downtown Pittsburgh. To the left was a larger waiting area, also lined with chairs, but large enough to have a central section of 6 chairs set back-to-back. There was a desk directly across the room from the entrance to this waiting room where a smiling woman sat. She looked to be in her 60's and was dressed in street clothes. As we entered the waiting room, she greeted us with a confident and gentle warmth. She informed us of the details of where we could wait and what there was to do. She also assured us that she would be there if we had any questions.

Stephanie's parents met us there a few minutes later. The earliness and the fear left us saying little to one another after the initial hellos and hugs.

Only moments after we sat down, a nurse called us in to the surgery prep room to see Samuel before surgery. Stephanie and I followed the nurses alone. We were escorted back down the hallway, past the elevators, and through the large oak doors that separated this small open section of the hospital from everything else. Just past the doors was the prep room. As we entered, we found our precious son lying on the first hospital bed to the left. He already had an IV, oxygen tubes in his nose, and had leads to all of his various monitors. The room was a pale green, almost a seafoam. It was open and had multiple places for hospital beds. The room was dimmed to a low light, which contrasted sharply with the intense hospital lights in hospital hallways. Wires, hookups, and IV poles, all connected to the wall (or waiting to be), stood behind each bed. Each waited solemnly for their next patient. We tearfully kissed our tiny son, prayed over him, and snuggled with him as close as we could while bending over a hospital bed. The anesthesiologist came and spoke with us briefly, his cheerful mood a helpful counterbalance to the heaviness we felt.

After a few minutes, the hospital staff directed us back to the waiting room so they could take Samuel back for surgery. The attendant took down our names and cell phones numbers, and she helped us find Samuel's number on one of the televisions used for listing each patient's status. The TV displayed a chart and alpha-numeric codes that looked more like stock tickers than the stages of where a patient was in the operating room.

The waiting room was well stocked with coffee, magazines, and televisions. The attendant informed us that if we wanted to sleep, the cardiac ICU waiting room was next door to the surgical waiting room. We were also told we could also wait there if we wanted, as it was smaller and usually quieter.

The four of us – Stephanie, her parents, and I - found ways to occupy ourselves, ways to keep our mind off the intensity of the situation and the major uneasiness we felt. We kept watch on the TV that had the ID numbers for each patient, each one a different child with an untold story. Eventually, the line that represented Samuel's status changed from one status update to the next. The words used to describe each status were supposed to be descriptive. Instead, they were very confusing. The first status change seemed to announce he was finished and in recovery, but he was actually in another stage of prep.

As we waited and watched, a hospital staff member would occasionally come to the attendant and ask for a parent. We sat numbly watching each time they came in to find a parent. I felt emotionally bound up; I was afraid to think through my fears and process any emotion. One might think we prayed, or sang worship songs, or any other thing we should do. We did none of that. We had prayed diligently up to this point for Samuel's protection, and we couldn't form words for anything else. We had nothing left to do but to wait; to painfully wait, knowing that our 2-1/2-month-old child was having open heart surgery a few hundred feet from where we sat. Stephanie and her parents watched TV, but I was restless. I tried playing games, and watching TV, and reading – everything that was available. I couldn't do any of it for very long.

Sometime in the early afternoon, an attendant came and found us.

"Are you Samuel's parents?" she said approaching us.

We nodded and replied, "Yes."

"He is through surgery and in recovery," she replied, "You can come see him."

We were all a little surprised, as his status still had not changed from what we were told was pre-surgery prep. Stephanie's Mom, Edith, looked at Stephanie and me, "Well, I guess he's done." We had just been discussing how his status hadn't change on the monitor.

Stephanie and I nodded, briefly looking at her and then back to the nurse. We were anxious to get to Samuel. Our eyes were locked forward as hurried to follow the nurse who had come to escort us.

We left the main waiting room, and turned to the left, which was the doorway into the other waiting room – the waiting room for the cardiac ICU. This room was square and had a huge window overlooking the city and the houses leading to downtown Pittsburgh. The walls were a dark red, with beige chairs and carpet. To the right of the door was a short hallway off the side of the room that led to the cardiac ICU, the left side of that hallway was the check-in where an attendant sat to let you in. We barely noticed the attendant or the large window and desk for the check in. The nurse led us through two more heavy double doors into the cardiac ICU, which was laid out like a giant square "C".

We followed the nurse to the first corner of the hallway. Samuel had a corner room with windows that faced Polish Hill and the Strip district. The white hallways were broken up by equipment on wheels, with black or grey cables hanging like vines of an overgrown jungle. The entire front wall of each room was made of two giant glass doors. Curtains covered those doors in most rooms, which were often darkened as patients lay recovering.

Samuel's room was bright white, as they had turned on the overhead lights and had the curtains open. Samuel lay sleeping. An oxygen mask covered his face, and a blanket covered his naked chest. Various tubes and lines ran from his tiny body to machines.

As soon as we saw him, we both rushed to his side. We were overjoyed that the surgery was over so quickly and were glad to see our son. Stephanie stroked his head and his cheek, standing on his right side. I stepped to his left side, smiling at him.

When Samuel's nurse entered, she filled us in on the details of his care and what she was doing with him.

"Why do they have him covered like that? What's with the

blanket?" my wife asked. The blanket covering Samuel's chest was pulled all the way to his chin.

"It's to cover him up," she replied, "They haven't closed his chest yet."

I was shocked.

Stephanie braved the same question I was thinking, "Why is that?"

Picture: Mommy and Samuel
http://www.rlshawver.com/ftcihp-pic2

"It's just a precaution," the nurse continued. "The doctors want to make sure there's no internal bleeding or problems. They have tubes running from his chest to pull out extra fluid."

With that answer, Stephanie and I were grateful for the blanket.

That evening we left Samuel to sleep in the CICU. Each room was incredibly well staffed. Nurses covered a maximum of two rooms, and in difficult cases or post op they only covered one. Samuel had one nurse that night, who never left his room.

The next morning when we entered, Samuel was awake. The instant he saw us, his smile lit up his whole face. It was so much brighter than the sun streaming in through the windows. There were so many unspoken fears up to this point, fears on which we refused to dwell. This is only a temporary fix, so what happens with the next surgery? What if he has complications? All of those fears dissipated with his radiant smile.

Thankfully, I had just finished my busy season at work and was able to devote a lot of time at the hospital to Stephanie and Samuel. However, I wasn't able to spend time with my older son, Izaiah, in those couple of weeks. Izaiah lived with his mom an hour and a half away from me. Samuel's surgery was on the weekend Izaiah was supposed to be with me, and I had skipped driving down to visit the week prior.

To get some time with him, I asked Izaiah's mom if it would be ok to come down on my Friday off, December 18th. It was 12 days after the surgery and less than a week before Christmas. She graciously agreed. That Friday, I left early in the morning so we could spend the day together. Izaiah had just turned 4 a few days earlier. To celebrate, I took him to a matinee to watch "Big Hero 6."

To our amazement, Izaiah and I had the theatre to ourselves that morning. I won't give away the plot of the movie, but there is a medical robot who becomes the protector and friend to the young star of the movie. The end has a strong emotional hook about sacrifice. I am grateful that Izaiah and I were the only ones in the theatre that day. While the last scene cut to the credits, I sat sobbing uncontrollably. All of the pent-up emotion of the last two weeks, all of my fears and frustrations – it all came pouring out as we sat in the darkened theatre. Izaiah was incredibly confused; he didn't seem to know how to respond to seeing his daddy cry like this. I cried until halfway through the credits when I was interrupted by a cut-scene. Once I had started crying, I was reluctant to stop. But the scene was both poignant and funny, and Izaiah and I both laughed. By the time we left the theatre, I felt lighter than I had felt in weeks.

CHAPTER 4

A NEW VALVE

"Even though I walk through the valley of the shadow of death... You are with me." ~ Psalm 23 NASB

Samuel came home from the hospital on Christmas Eve. The next day, at 2:00 P.M., we met Izaiah's Mom in Morgantown to pick Izaiah up, so he could spend the week of Christmas with us. There wasn't much celebration that Christmas; we were all still in shock. But at least we were able to be together as a family. Thankfully, we like putting our tree up just after Thanksgiving and buying our gifts early. Christmas decorating and shopping were finished before Samuel went into the hospital, or else we wouldn't have had anything for Izaiah under our tree.

While we celebrated the holidays at home, Samuel recovered. He did not seem to be affected by the surgery after the first few days. Stephanie and I took most of the time between Christmas off work, and we were grateful for the rest. In my morning Bible readings that week, I came across a passage in 2 Chronicles 20 that greatly encouraged me. We knew that this surgery was just the beginning, and that there would be more struggles ahead.

In the passage, three separate armies joined together to wage war against King Jehoshaphat and the Kingdom of Judah. Judah was an incredibly small Kingdom, made up of two of the twelve tribes of Israel that had split from the other ten. The people were incredibly outnumbered. These people who now gathered to slaughter them had often been their allies. In desperation, the king called for a fast. A prophecy came to the prophet Jahaziel, and one line in particular resonated with me. The prophecy went like this:

> *Do not be afraid or discouraged because of this vast army. For the battle is not yours, but God's. Tomorrow march down against them. They will be climbing up by the Pass of Ziz, and you will find them at the end of the gorge in the Desert of Jeruel. ¹⁷ You will not have to fight this battle. Take up your positions; stand firm and see the deliverance the* LORD *will give you, Judah and Jerusalem. Do not be afraid; do not be discouraged. Go out to face them tomorrow, and the* LORD *will be with you. 2 Chron 20:16b-17*

The line that stuck out to me was this, "For the battle is not yours, but God's." The Spirit of the Lord was giving me encouragement, and a promise on which I could stand. He didn't tell me that it was for me, I just knew. This was God's way of telling me that He would be fighting these battles for me, so I added this to my confession.

As we finished celebrating the holidays and moved into the new year, my desire to return to my normal was overshadowed by a serious disagreement with Izaiah's mom. Unfortunately, this continued for the next few months. Stephanie's work still required her to work in the office, and mine required an extreme level of dedication and mental focus. On top of all this, I had been actively building my Amway business right up until the point Samuel had entered the hospital.

burned to get back to building my Amway business. Instead, I became consumed in the fight with Izaiah's mom.

As the cold month of January and the new year began, we knew in the back of our minds that the stitch in Samuel's heart valve was a temporary fix. We knew it would not last long, but we also had no idea what that meant.

In the meantime, Samuel continued to grow and develop normally. I continued my early morning routine of waking early and

Video: Samuel smiling
http://www.rlshawver.com/ftcihp-vid8

reading my Bible before work. Some mornings, Samuel was awake, or Stephanie would be awake giving him a bottle and changing his diaper. Occasionally, I would give her a break so I could have the opportunity to snuggle with him before work. In those first few months, the development of a baby is so rapid, and everything new they do is so incredibly special. With Samuel, the awe was compounded by the gravity of his situation.

In the beginning of March, the situation with Izaiah's Mom was still raging as my focus. It all took a huge turn when I stumbled across a section of the third book Jake had recommended to me, "The Power of a Praying Parent," by Stormie O'Martian. One chapter applied specifically to the situation we were facing. I prayed the suggested prayer – changing only the names. Within a few weeks, we found out the situation was remedied … on the day I prayed that prayer.

A few days later, Stephanie noticed that Samuel wasn't eating well. After one day of this, she called his pediatrician to see what should be done. Given Samuel's history, the pediatrician encouraged Stephanie to take him to Children's hospital, just to be safe.

It was Wednesday, March 11th. It was a few hours after I had come home from work when the doctor finally gave us the go-ahead to take him down. This time, we took the quicker route to Children's, down through Millvale. We eventually turned into the emergency room entrance, which is located on the side of the hospital. The entrance curved up under the overhanging third floor, with a cement barrier separating the entrance to the underground ER parking garage.

The bright fluorescent lights and the white hallway behind the sliding glass doors offset the grey cement of the supporting structure of the building and the darkness outside. I pulled Stephanie's SUV in and stopped in front of the doors. She hopped out, detached Samuel's carrier from the car seat base, and carried him in through the doors. I parked the car.

After parking, and riding the elevators up from the garage, I made the right towards the Emergency Room entrance. The hospital lobby opened to the right as I made my way to the security desk. I unpacked my pockets, stepped through the metal detectors, and found my wife.

Thankfully, the hospital seemed to understand the need for swiftness. Within minutes of me finding Stephanie sitting in a chair with Samuel beside her, the nurses called Samuel's name. We were then whisked to a small screening area where we went over Samuel's history and the nurse checked his vitals. Stephanie told the nurse how he wasn't eating well, and they went over our insurance information.

The hospital staff then sent us back into the main waiting room. We sat for only a few moments before they called us back to the main rooms. We passed through the double doors with our usual parental load: Samuel in his baby carrier, my book bag, and Samuel's diaper bag which doubled as Stephanie's purse. Through the double oak doors, we made a right and wove through the labyrinth of hallways, eventually ending up at a small grey triage room.

We took Samuel out of his carrier and placed him on the bed. A nurse began hooking him up to the heart monitor while a tech came by to get our insurance information and history, again. We gave her the run down, as the other nurse checked him over. The nurse eventually informed us that Samuel was once again in SVT – his heart was beating at over 200 beats per minute.

Soon after the tech left; the doctor assigned to Samuel gave us the rundown. He described to us of the typical techniques of how to get a baby out of SVT. We were in a fog – everyone was moving so fast. We were growing more concerned with everyone's serious demeanor and swiftness of action. It was a struggle to keep up both mentally and physically.

The doctor went on to describe that one of the easiest ways is to "shock" the baby, by grabbing them by their ankles and jerking them quickly into the air or cradling them in your arms and laying them backwards towards their head rapidly.

The doctor tried this method once or twice, but it did not seem to affect Samuel. He then left the room to discuss other options with the rest of the staff. I continued to try pulling him up by his ankles while praying, asking God to make Samuel's heart go back to a normal rhythm. I prayed anxiously as I grabbed him by his ankles and pulled him up into the air. While he seemed somewhat startled by all of this, it wasn't enough to bring him back into a normal rhythm.

The doctor returned a few minutes later. They had decided to attempt to break Samuel's SVT by stopping his heart with medication. Stephanie and I were concerned, but we were also in way over our heads, so we just nodded in agreement. Soon a swarm of doctors and nurses entered our room. There were too many people moving around to see what was happening, so we waited patiently as they worked on our 5-month-old baby, attempting to comfort him and each other around the mass of professionals. On the first try, his heart began beating normally. Stephanie and I felt an immediate relief of the tension in the room. We rested, and eventually Samuel was admitted to a room on the 7th floor. He spent a week in the hospital, as they upped his doses of medication to keep his heart from breaking its normal rhythm.

When we returned home, Stephanie continued to struggle with getting Samuel to eat. We noticed he was losing his baby fat and starting to look gaunt. After struggling for another week, we took him back to Children's Hospital.

When the nurses checked his vitals, we realized that Samuel was once again in SVT. They moved Samuel on to a room in the ER, this time a small inner room with an adult bed. When the doctor on staff arrived, she discussed once again the methods of breaking his SVT. We nodded in agreement.

I chimed in, "After we realized Samuel was in SVT, I went ahead and tried to get him out of it by grabbing him by the ankles and flipping him upside down."

The doctor paused and looked at me as if I had a third eye. She shook her head and continued, "We typically try to break a child out of SVT by taking a bag of ice and putting it over their face."

Stephanie and I nodded in agreement thinking that the doctor new best. We were confused why the first method was bad, but we went along with it.

The doctor already had the ice ready. We got the impression she wasn't concerned with our approval, as she proceeded to aggressively place a plastic bag filled with ice on his face, which completely covered Samuel's head. He was already very unhappy with the unfamiliar environment, and he proceeded to scream and thrash violently. While this shocked Samuel, it did not succeed in getting his heart rhythm to reset.

Stephanie gasped and attempted to comfort him as much as possible, while he screamed behind the bag of ice. I stood by their sides, trying to comfort them both. We steeled ourselves, hoping that this would pull him out of SVT. I continued praying that his SVT would break.

When it didn't work the first time, the doctor attempted it again. Stephanie and I both cringed as Samuel screamed and writhed violently. It still didn't work.

After the second attempt, she gratefully decided to switch to chemically stopping Samuel's heart. They ran through the same procedure as Samuel's last trip to the ER, hooking him up with 18 leads to an EKG. This time, the team was smaller, and Stephanie and I could see the process better. When the doctor left the room, and a nurse and a tech stayed. They placed each of the stickers and attached each EKG lead to the metal buttons on the stickers. When they finished getting everything placed, they filled two syringes. They filled the smaller of the two with the medicine, and the larger with saline solution. After these tasks, the two stopped and began to chat. After a few moments, we politely asked what the delay was. The nurse informed us that they were waiting on the doctor to return.

After an uncomfortable amount of time, the doctor finally came back in the room. The doctor took the large syringe, and the nurse took the small one. On a 3 count, they tag team injected the Adenosine and the saltwater flush into his IV. His heart monitor flatlined momentarily, and then switched to a normal rhythm.

Stephanie and I relaxed, knowing he was back in a normal heartbeat pattern. We keyed off the doctor's stress, and their urgency to get Samuel's heart beating normally parlayed the same sense of urgency to us.

Within a few minutes, however, Samuel's heart monitor beeped twice. We looked up at the monitor, only to see that he was back in SVT.

The doctor's administered a second dose while I prayed that he would stay out of SVT.

As we sat in the hospital room, waiting breathlessly, and hoping his heart rate wouldn't jump back into its double time rhythm, a recent memory popped into my head.

My granddad, who we affectionately called Big-Nan Daddy or Bing Daddy (when I was too small to say Big Nan Daddy) had an arrhythmia. It worsened around the same time as Samuel's first surgery, and they had to administer Adenosine to him to stop his heart in order to break it out of an arrhythmia. My mom had related the events on the phone to me when it happened. She worried out loud about the fact that they were literally stopping his heart, and that something could go wrong with that process. My mom has always been prone to fretting over things that could go wrong. The memory broke through the fog– they were stopping Samuel's heart.

As I sat in that room with my arm around my wife, next to my 6-month-old son lying on a gurney, I tried to push the thoughts aside. The doctors were doing what they had to do to save our son.

Samuel was eventually admitted into the hospital and put in the cardiac ward, 7A, where they began the dance of trying to regulate his heartbeat with medications. The doctors decided to add a second medicine to the mix, hoping that by spacing out the two they could get better coverage.

That weekend was a whirlwind of activity, with Stephanie staying at the hospital with Samuel and me running back and forth while sleeping alone in our bed at home.

On Sunday, I attended church. I needed to be out of the hospital. I needed to be around the people in our church. I draw strength from getting around other believers and connecting. When the service was over, I stuck around in the auditorium with a smile on my face, hoping to find someone with whom I could connect. I had a few decent conversations, but none that were long enough to allow me to verbally process what was happening.

Feeling somewhat satisfied, but not fully, I left church and drove to the hospital. I parked, checked in, and made my way up to Samuel's room through the various hallways.

The walls of Samuel's hospital room glowed yellow in the afternoon sunlight, which matched the light oak cabinets in the room. Samuel's crib was against the wall to the right of the door when I walked in, and the futon where Stephanie slept was on the left.

When I arrived, Stephanie was visibly upset.

"Babe, what's wrong?" I asked, her posture conveyed that she was deeply worried.

"He's still not eating," she replied, "and he's starting to look worse."

I knew there was more she wanted to say, but I wasn't sure how to get it out of her and she didn't offer. I could tell she knew there was more wrong than she could verbalize. I walked over to look at Samuel in his crib; he had become incredibly thin in the past few weeks. He looked significantly worse than the night before. On top of his skinniness, there was a tinge of yellow to his skin.

My wife spoke up as I looked him over, "He ate less than an ounce last night, and that's all he would take. I can't get him to take anything else."

I nodded, continuing to look him over. I grabbed Steph's hand and prayed out loud for his safety, and then we sat in silence for a few moments.

"Have you spoken to the doctors about it?" I asked.

"I spoke to the nurses," she replied. "They don't seem to think it's a big deal."

The room we were in on 7C faced north and looked out onto a rooftop and the red brick wall of a different part of the hospital. The sun, streaming through the curtains, gave the room that lazy Sunday feel – it was oblivious to the intense fear we felt. I sat next to my wife on her hospital room futon. We were scared, and we knew there was no way a child could continue like this for long.

I did the best I could to comfort my wife as she again tried feeding him from a bottle. Finally, after multiple attempts, he took an ounce of formula. For his age, this is the equivalent of and adult eating a quarter of a sandwich. I hoped that him eating something meant Stephanie was worrying too much.

Soon after, when he filled his diaper, my fears grew to match Stephanie's. Samuel's poop wasn't normal; it resembled dried milk chunks or cottage cheese. His body wasn't even able to process the formula we were giving him. It felt like he was dying, like we were losing our son. There was a somber fatigue that hung heavy over both of us.

But I wouldn't go down without swinging.

I rang the call button and asked the nurse to put us in contact with Samuel's doctors. Despite Stephanie's previous attempts, I wasn't going to take no for an answer. Since Children's is a teaching hospital, we often had to go through a head nurse, and then a resident, and then a fellow before we could speak directly with Samuel's doctors: Dr. Arora or Dr. Beerman.

Samuel's nurse entered within a few moments. "What can I do for you, she said with a smile."

Taking a firm but gentle tone, I replied, "We are really concerned about Samuel. He's not eating, and he doesn't look good. We would like to speak to one of Samuel's doctors."

"We don't think it's that big of a deal. They checked him out earlier this weekend," she stated, gently trying to brush off our concern.

"I understand," I said in a gentle concession, "But we would like to speak to them anyway." I looked her directly in the eye, not wanting to be mean, but also refusing to say no.

She sighed, "Ok, I'll page them."

I eventually managed to speak on the phone to a Fellow, who promised to get in touch with Dr. Arora, Samuel's Electrophysiologist.

Eventually the fellow came down to look Samuel over. After making some calls, they decided to take Samuel up to the cardiac ICU. We settled ourselves and our few belongings into the new room on the 4th floor. I eventually left to go home. I shot a quick text to my boss, telling him that I was taking sick time tomorrow. I needed to be at the hospital. My wife needed me there to fight beside her for Samuel's health. I also shot a text to Jake to ask for prayer for Samuel, and to update him that he wasn't doing so well.

Jake replied with more verses from the Bible – verses that promised God's healing. I looked them up the first moment I had.

The next day, Dr. Morell (Samuel's surgeon from his first surgery) came by to speak with us.

We laid out our list of concerns, just as we had to every doctor and resident prior to him. As we spoke, he looked at the floor with his hand on his chin, listening intently. He nodded at the end of each statement, making it obvious he was taking it in. When we finished, he looked up and paused momentarily, looking us directly in the eye. With a wave of the hand that had been holding his chin, he said in his slight South American accent, "No problem. We'll do the surgery."

We were relieved. The concerns of a new surgery seemed miniscule in the face of seeing our son look so bad.

The doctors deemed Samuel just large enough for an artificial heart valve. He was six months old. There are multiple sizes of heart valve available, and the doctors had a small mechanical valve they hoped would be just the right size to replace Samuel's mitral valve. Going forward, this meant he would have to be on blood thinners in addition to the barrage of heart regulation medications he was being given to control his SVT. But at this point, we accepted all of it as necessity and prepped for the mental weight of a second open heart surgery.

That next morning was a Tuesday, March 16th. I rose early as I always do to spend time reading my Bible and writing down the verses that spoke to me. My heart was heavy, and fear threatened to overtake me.

I had slept in the hospital with Stephanie and Samuel. After searching out coffee, I found a chair overlooking the city. Coffee in hand, I carefully wrote out every word of Psalms 112. Each stroke of my pen was a release. I sought out the passage that had formed my main confession, the one that I confessed over him every single night. As I slowly pressed my fears into God's word, each word slowly brought release to the tension I felt in my soul.

"Praise the Lord. Blessed are those who fear the Lord, who find great delight in His commands. Their children will be mighty in the land, the generation of the upright will be blessed." Psalms 112:1-2 NIV

I typically wrote only the verses that meant something; but this morning, I needed every word. My 6-month-old son was about to undergo a second open heart surgery and to replace his heart valve, and the weight of my anxiety lay heavy on my spirit. Growing up, my parents often shared stories of people who died because of anesthesia or from complication during surgery. These anxieties added to the weight of my already burdened soul. How many people had I heard pass away in heart surgery?

I continued writing out God's word.

"...4 Even in the darkness light dawns for the upright, for those who are gracious and compassionate and righteous...6 Surely the righteous will never be shaken; they will be remembered forever." Psalms 112:4, 6 NIV

The words settled my soul.

I finished my reading and journaling and went to prepare for the day. Transport eventually came to take Samuel down to surgical prep. We walked with them. When we made it to the surgical preparation room, Stephanie and I prayed over Samuel as we had the first time. We then made our way to the waiting room.

Again, Stephanie's parents met us in the waiting room that morning. While I occasionally feel the urge to think that I should have prayed through the entire surgery, we had already prayed and already thanked God that Samuel would be safe. I didn't need to beg God. We would not be shaken. At this point we had been praying over Samuel for months. We asked God, and I knew He was going to keep Samuel safe.

As we sat waiting for the surgery to end, Stephanie and her parents watched television. I was a little more antsy. I flitted from reading a book, to playing a board game, to grabbing another cup of coffee.

The operation stretched through lunch, and I went with Steph's parents to grab food at the cafeteria. Stephanie wanted to stay in case the doctors returned. We ate and then brought her up hot food.

We had been keeping an eye on the screen that showed the status of every child's surgery. As before, the code that represented Samuel would change color as he moved through each part of the surgery. The text next to Samuel's code had changed a few times to notify us that he was first going into prep, and then leaving prep. The status saying Samuel was leaving prep was the longest, and it stretched on until the afternoon.

Finally, a nurse came out to tell us that he was in recovery. They ushered Stephanie and I through the doors into the same cardiac ICU room he had been in earlier. As this was his second open heart surgery, we knew a little more of what to expect, and Samuel already looked better. The new valve was enabling his heart to pump blood healthily through his body. His color wasn't as yellow or as pale, and he had a tinge of the healthy pink color we knew so well.

They thankfully hid his open chest under the blanket. We had an idea of what was under the white blanket with a blue and pink stripe at the end, as a tube that was obviously used for drainage from underneath it to a storage container below his bed. None of the array of monitors and tubes registered to us as to what they were doing. All we really saw was that our baby boy was looking healthier, and we were thankful.

CHAPTER 5

THE PICC LINE

"WHOEVER FEARS THE LORD HAS A SECURE FORTRESS, AND FOR THEIR CHILDREN IT WILL BE A REFUGE." ~ PSALM 14:26 NIV

Samuel's weakness coming into surgery made for a difficult recovery. After his first surgery, he was off the bipap – which is a full-face oxygen mask – before we came in to see him. He was awake and alert by the next day, if a little groggy. He progressed quickly and was back on the 7th floor in a few days.

After heart surgeries, fluid will often get inside the lungs because the bypass machine isn't as effective as the heart itself. There are also fluids in and around the chest cavity that needs to clear. A normal and healthy person's lungs and heart clear these fluids naturally.

After this second surgery, Samuel was still asleep after 36 hours, wearing a bipap. To make matters worse, instead of clearing the fluid from his lungs and around his chest quickly, he was going backwards by gaining more fluid in his lungs.

Up to that point, we had been praying, and asking others to pray that Samuel would recover quickly, but that wasn't happening. We were alarmed. That evening I asked God why Samuel wasn't recovering. I didn't even ask it out loud. It was just an unspoken, cry of the heart, prayer as we went to get dinner in the hospital cafeteria. "God, why aren't You acting?" Almost immediately, I felt a strong sense in my spirit, a tug at my heart and a whisper in my spirit. "You should pray for the specific thing you need." Suddenly, I remembered a teaching Jake had given at our last business conference about goals and how they needed to be small and measurable.

From that moment forward, we started praying specifically about the next step in Samuel's recovery. I didn't even tell Stephanie, but she picked up on how I was praying immediately. We began praying that God would remove the extra fluid from Samuel's chest cavity, and that He would help Samuel's heart to process it. We asked others to pray for the same things.

Video: Samuel in the CICU
http://www.rlshawver.com/ftcihp-vid1

Overnight, Samuel's body cleared the fluids from his chest.

We then began to pray the next step to Samuel's healing, that he would be off the bipap machine. We prayed that he would be able to breathe well, and his lungs would heal. Within 48 hours, Samuel was no longer wearing the bipap machine. Although progress was slow for Samuel's recovery, we still prayed him forward ... Every step of the way, God swiftly answered our specific prayer.

Eventually, Samuel started to return to his smiling and strong self.

Samuel spent close to ten days in the CICU before the medical staff transferred Samuel up a floor to the pediatric ICU, or the PICU. They needed the extra space in the cardiac ICU for more children pre- or post-operation. Samuel was recovering well but wasn't quite ready for a room on the main floor. As Samuel's healing progressed, I returned to my normal work schedule. Stephanie decided to skip work for the week, taking the last of her off time.

She never left Samuel's side, unless there was someone else there with him.

The PICU was much larger than the CICU. It had multiple units and a few different nursing stations laid out along the length of the hospital. In contrast, the CICU had approximately ten rooms in a blocky "C", arrayed around a single large central medical station. In the PICU, Samuel stayed in the cluster of rooms at the second nursing station to the east, or the left if you were walking through the PICU entrance. The walls in the hallway were a warmer color, almost a pink or a salmon, and there were lots of windows. After hours, however, the hallways seemed very dark. The night sky, combined with the lights of downtown Pittsburgh, seemed to overpower the overhead lights. I assumed they dimmed the lights in the corridors so the children could sleep.

Two weeks after the second surgery, I was back in my normal routine. I woke at 5:30 AM so I could read my Bible. I would then shower and arrive at work at 7 a.m. For my lunch hour, I would go out to network to find prospective business partners to expand my Amway business. At 5 p.m., I would leave work and drive through the city in rush hour traffic to the hospital, hoping to have dinner with Stephanie and Samuel.

Every other Thursday, I would leave work and drive 90 minutes to see Izaiah in Morgantown. On Tuesdays, I would eat dinner with Stephanie and Samuel, and then leave at 7 p.m. I would then drive back west for a meeting with my local business partners. I typically arrived around 7:30. I would chat with my friends and business associates for ten or twenty minutes before the meeting started, which gave me the chance to work with any new prospects I had. If I hadn't chosen to invite any prospects or if they didn't show, I took the time to chat with my friends and be encouraged by their presence. I thrived off of this team. Their positivity uplifted and encouraged me in my fight. Their faith in their future, and in their Maker, were pillars that kept me focused.

The meeting would start promptly at 8:00 PM, where the local leaders of our business team shared the marketing plan to new prospects. This Tuesday, two and a half weeks after Samuel's heart valve replacement, I had sat down in the back of the room to listen to Jon speak. I had no prospective business partners that night, so I sat on the second row from the back. At ten minutes after eight, I received a text from Stephanie saying, "Call me!!"

I excused myself from the room, bringing my things with me in case I needed to leave. I quietly closed one of the double doors behind me in the back of the room and hit send on her number. She answered the phone in hysterics, "Something happened to Samuel.... His eyes rolled back up into his head.... He started jerking!" she said breathlessly, pausing frantically between each short sentence. She was so upset I could barely understand her, and despite the pauses, she was talking so quickly that I couldn't grasp what she was saying.

"What?" I questioned, trying to get her to slow down.

"He started convulsing. His eyes rolled up in his head. He did it a few times."

"I'll head right down. Let me call you back," I said.

I gave a quick goodbye to my friends manning the doors that night, hopped into my car, and sped back to Children's Hospital.

I arrived on the 5th floor to the entrance of the PICU. I hit the buzzer at the door and waited to be allowed to enter. The electronic lock clicked, and I pulled opened the heavy wooden doors. I am not sure if I noticed anyone sitting at the first desk as I passed quickly through the hallways to Samuel's room. I assumed that the person who let me in must be at a different desk. I hurried through the first unit and past the desk for the second unit.

When I made it to Samuel's room, Stephanie began filling me in on the details. "They think Samuel had multiple strokes," she said, much more calmly than before. A nurse was checking Samuel, and she made her way in and out of the room as Stephanie filled me in on the rest of the details.

My jaw dropped as the thought passed through my head, "Aren't strokes what old people have?" Instead of saying it aloud, I simply asked, "What?", hoping I had misheard.

Stephanie continued, "Yeah, it's ok. He hasn't had any more since, and they are going to do a full battery of tests. He must have had a clot pass to his brain."

"How did that happen?" I mumbled, shocked. How could my son have had multiple strokes? My mind wasn't processing what had happened.

Stephanie shook her head, "Well, I've been trying to get them to put a second PICC line in to test his heparin."

From there, I settled in to find out the rest of the details.

It is standard during heart surgeries, and other intense surgical procedures to insert a PICC line, which is also called a central line.

It's similar to an IV, but it is placed in the neck or chest and goes directly to the heart. When someone has a mechanical valve surgically implanted in their heart, they must put the patient on an IV blood thinner called Heparin. The mechanical valve can cause clotting as the blood cells pass through, and the blood thinners work to keep that from happening. The standard medication is Coumadin, also known as Warfarin, and is taken in a pill form. However, Coumadin takes a few days to build up in the system. While it is hitting what they call "therapeutic" levels in the blood, the medical staff uses a quicker acting blood thinner called Heparin to "bridge" the patient onto the Coumadin.

Since Samuel was only 6 months old, administering something that is typically an adult medicine required a large amount of precision. The nurses would take the feeding line off his PICC line, flush it, and then draw blood out of the same port. Stephanie informed me that they were having problems doing things this way. Every time they tested his Heparin levels, he was showing incredibly high numbers. They would stop the drip, and then wait for forty-five minutes. When they tested him again, he was showing extremely low levels and they would rush to get him back on the Heparin drip.

Stephanie noticed the pattern after the first few times doing this and realized they were not getting good readings after they flushed his line. She knew they needed to do something else, and she had been requesting that they insert a second PICC line so they could get a good reading. The nurses taking the readings kept brushing off her suggestions, saying that a second PICC line would put him at too much risk. A PICC line, they reasoned, was prone to infection and a second would be double the chances of infection. Because they kept testing in this manner, Samuel's Heparin levels were continuously dropping too low. Eventually, with Samuel's blood not being properly thinned by the heparin, his mechanical valve caused a blood clot that went straight to his brain, which is what causes a stroke.

After I was fully caught up on the back story, I went into action mode. I turned to the first nurse and insisted that they listen to my wife and insert another PICC line. That, I acquiesced, or take some other method of testing him to keep this from happening again. When the nurse said no, I asked for the resident. The resident insisted that wasn't possible. I wasn't backing down.

Seeing that I wasn't willing to stop, a male lead nurse took me aside. He was in his late twenties and just under six feet tall. He was fairly thin, with blonde hair. He had the arrogance of a young man who's been promoted without having to deal with the major difficulties and disappointments of life. I'm not sure if he felt that my firm tone of voice meant I was a threat, or if he felt that he needed to "state the facts" in a way I could understand.

He led me down the hallway to a short cubby hole that had a window situated in between PICU units. This was the most private place he could find without leaving the PICU.

"Hey big guy. Listen, they aren't going to do another PICC line for your son," he said after squaring up to me.

I stared at him, giving him the small smile I give when I know I need to use people skills to not tell someone they are stupid.

I wasn't sure why this guy had pulled me aside, but I stood politely waiting for him to finish. I knew in the back of my mind that this guy wasn't going to help me and that I needed to get away from him to find someone who could help.

"It's just not common procedure. I have worked here at this hospital for a couple years and I have never seen anyone do that," he continued.

I started trying to turn and walk away, "Listen, I need to go be with my wife and my son."

Sensing this tactic was not working, he tried changing the subject. He continued the conversation by talking about his experience level in the hospital and listing all of his qualifications. While he droned on, I kept smiling through gritted teeth.

At some point he must have realized I wasn't listening intently enough, so he switched subjects. He began to ask questions about our family. My faith was always at the forefront of my mind because I was in the heat of battle, and my faith was my weapon. God's Word was my sword, He was my fortress, and we were under siege. Thinking he was ready to listen, I began to talk about my faith.

When I noticed his interest in what I had to say, I made mention of how I sang worship songs over Samuel. When he asked which ones, I mentioned "Oceans" by Hillsong United, because that had been the most prominent.

Thinking that I might have the opportunity to share what God was doing in my life, I started to get excited. It was cut short. Before I could add another sentence, he interrupted "Oh, I know that song. I can play it on my guitar," he interjected as I took a breath between sentences.

I nodded and winced ever so slightly at the interruption.

"Yeah, I play it with the worship band at my church." I knew the church he was talking. I am not incredibly fond of said church. The leadership has been guilty of publicly criticizing people who have impacted me on my faith journey. From my experience, these environments seem to succeed well at breeding arrogant people.

"Figures," I thought. I was done with the conversation.

As he continued talking about his church, I tuned him out completely and decided it was time to leave. Sticking out one hand for a handshake and putting my other on his shoulder, I said, "Hey man, I'm sorry to cut you short, but I really need to get back to my wife."

Shocked at the sudden interruption to the monologue he thought was going so well, he shook my hand in shock. As he stood with his mouth half open, I pushed past him before he had a chance to stop me.

I marched back to Samuel's room to find my wife.

The hospital's incompetence was the reason my son had multiple strokes, and their "standard procedure" was the cause. I wasn't looking for retaliation. I only wanted my son to be healthy and whole.

Once I made it back in the room, I had Steph catch me up on what I had missed. I rejoined her in continuing to press for a second PICC line for Samuel. Finally, one of the fellows, a young woman named Sam, agreed that a second PICC line made sense.

They put in a second PICC line within a few hours.

We learned a hard lesson that day on how vital it is to advocate for your loved ones in medical care, and how incredibly important it is to stick by your guns. Most of my life I had been taught how important it was to listen to the experts. I was realizing that sometimes a mom is the best expert on her child. Unfortunately, Samuel's strokes weren't the only consequences of their missteps.

The initial battery of tests they ran on Samuel showed his brain function to be fine and that there was no long-term damage.

Two weeks later, the doctors performed an echocardiogram in order to check his heart function. During this test, they take sonographic pictures of the heart chambers and valves. With it, they can measure the pressure gradient across the artificial valve. Unfortunately, a clot had propped one of the mechanical leaflets open. Samuel's heart valve was not working properly. The doctors informed us he would need immediate heart surgery to replace the clotted valve. Less than a month after Samuel's first mechanical valve was put in, it was already getting replaced.

I was beginning to crack. Between the hospital visits, juggling my work schedule, trying to find time for my older son, being away from my wife, and all of Samuel's medical procedures, I was hurting. The pressure was taking a heavy toll on me. Stephanie was trying to get hours in at work and dealing with the constant barrage of hospital visits. It was during this period that God spoke to Stephanie. She felt Him tell her that Samuel was going to be ok.

It was only March, but I was running out of sick time and vacation, which had rolled over in January. Despite the circumstances of my home life, there were plenty of tasks at my job that I was expected to perform at full quality. Samuel's situation was not an excuse for me to not perform.

One of those tasks is an economic evaluation of the entire region of the company. I was in the middle of this evaluation by myself when all of this was happening - the strokes and the first and second mitral valve replacement. In some ways, the work was a pleasant respite. It provided a way for me to focus all of my energy on the tasks at hand and shut out all of the craziness.

On the other hand, the schedules and the pressure were exhausting me. Samuel had come through this third surgery fine, but he looked weak and gaunt. All of the pinkness of his skin that had returned after the first surgery was gone. The hope that this was a positive turning point now seemed so far away. We were afraid before his first heart valve replacement that he was dying. We weren't afraid he was dying anymore, but he still looked exceptionally weak. The extremely long recovery after his last surgery weighed heavily on our minds. Was it going to be three more weeks for him to recover? We were so exhausted we couldn't figure out how to verbalize our concerns. There was only heaviness.

The day of the third surgery was a blur. When I entered Samuel's room after his operation, however, everything came into rapidly into focus.

As Stephanie and I entered his CICU room, we weren't blessed with that blanket that covered his chest after his first and second surgery. The blanket was off, and we could see where his chest was split open. It was covered with a large piece of plastic tape, which more resembled the size and consistency of a thick Saran wrap. A tube protruded out from under the propped open half of his rib cage, right at the midpoint of his sternum. His sternum would soon be wired shut, as it had been after every other surgery, but for now it was split down the center. As I looked at my son, I felt a sense of panic.

In my morning reading, I had been spending a lot of the Old Testament section of the Bible. I found several God's promise from studying this section. I was also reading of the battles and the brutality of the wars to establish the young nation of Israel and keep its people alive. With all wars, the collateral damage is the family. For the Israelites, if their warriors failed in their battle to defend their country, the women were taken for slaves and the young children were brutally murdered.

For a brief instant, I saw Samuel, laying in the dirt. He was in the exact same position as in his hospital bed – flat on his back, head rolled to his right side, propped up slightly. Instead of the hospital level of cleanliness, he had dust on him, and he looked exactly as he did now with his chest cut open, gaunt and pale. The small amount of caked blood from his operation combined with the split down his chest enhanced the vision of feeling he had been brutally murdered. His small lifeless body lie on the hospital bed, but for a moment in my mind, he was dead.

Thankfully, the fearful vision lasted for only a moment.

"No," I whispered, regaining my composure. "God has promised in His word that Samuel will live long in the land and grow strong in the land." I said it quietly, so no one outside of the room would hear it.

The racing line on his heart monitor, drawing steep mountains and flat lines, echoed my confession. Samuel was alive.

During this time, Stephanie's Mom had also laid claim to God's promise that he "will surely live and not die," as it proclaims in Psalm 118:17 (NIV).

I continued to whisper both confessions as I stood staring at his lifeless body lying on the hospital bed.

As I drew closer to him, I reassured myself, "God's promises are true. He *does* protect the children of the righteous." One verse I had stumbled across in my morning readings, resonated along those same lines:

"Whoever fears the LORD has a secure fortress, and for their children it will be a refuge." ~ Proverbs 14:26 NIV

As I stood beside Samuel, I leaned down to get close and gently brushed his hair with my whole hand. I felt the warmth from his skin. As I leaned over my handsome boy, the last remnants of the shakiness from the vision left me. I wanted to touch him to reassure him with my presence, but his presence reassured me. The enemy had not won. Samuel would live long in the land and grow strong in the land.

CHAPTER 6

A SUMMER OF PERSONAL GROWTH

"The LORD directs the steps of the godly. He delights in every detail of their lives. Though He may stumble, he will not fall, for the LORD upholds him with his hand"
– Psalm 37:23 NLT

WSamuel's recovery with this second heart valve was nothing like his recovery after the prior surgery. Within a week after this surgery, he was back on the 7th floor, smiling as if he hadn't a care in the world. Our only hiccup was one major bout with SVT ten days after surgery. Because of this, Samuel had to go back to the

Picture: Samuel grinning in the Baby Carrier
http://www.rlshawver.com/ftcihp-pic3

ICU for the night to monitor his progress on the new combination of medications to regulate his heart rate. Within two weeks of this third surgery, which replaced his heart valve for the second time, we were heading home.

When we left the hospital, Samuel was on the max dosage of three different heart regulating medications. In the hospital, the nurses were administering his medications every four hours. Upon discharge, they had given us paperwork stating that we should continue the same four-hour rotation.

After thinking this through, I encouraged Stephanie to consult the doctors on switching to an 8-hour schedule. It's difficult to get a good night's rest with a baby in the house. Being forced to wake up every 4 hours would put a lot more stress on both of us. I thought it was noble that Stephanie wanted to try, but she would have to do so largely on her own. The nurses had a team – at home it was just the two of us, and I wasn't much help because of the heavy burden of my job.

Stephanie brushed off my concerns, insisting she could do it. I admired her courage, but after two days, she realized the schedule was already taking a heavy toll on her. She called the doctor on call that evening and was able to get approval to put him on an 8-hour schedule.

For the next seven months, we were graced with relative calm. Things slowed at my work to a more normal pace, as was typical during the summer. Samuel had no surgeries or life-threatening incidents. With Samuel getting older, and his rate of growth less extreme - the doctors had a more stable target for effectively dosing him with the proper meds. Even our visits to the hospital, to break Samuel out of SVT and readjust his medications, tapered down to once every other month.

The calm was needed. Stephanie and I spent the time recovering mentally from the exhaustion. Samuel spent the time recovering and catching up on cognitive development he had missed. The Holy Spirit spent the time preparing me for the battle ahead.

In the calm, I began to question one of my beliefs. I was addressing a doubt that had popped up during the last month of surgeries, one that I didn't have time to deal with at the time, since Samuel was in the midst of his surgeries. Could I just lay claim to any promise in the Bible?

All of God's promises in the Old Testament are hinged on our righteousness – our right standing with God - or at least some aspect of that. I know now that our salvation guarantees us all of God's promises. In this period, though, I didn't know if I was able to fulfill all of the intricate requirements for some of the promises on which I was standing. I was beginning to wonder whether the promises of the Old Testament were for me, and for Samuel.

Deep down, I knew God's promises had to be available for me. God wasn't a God who would tease me with goodness only to withhold it for someone else. In the same sense, I had no idea where to start in creating a solid, biblically backed case for this belief. My entire faith for Samuel's healing and survival hung on knowing that I could trust the goodness of God. In my mind, I asked myself, "Why would a God who claims to be good tease me by sharing His promises, only to hide somewhere in the details that I didn't qualify?" When people hide escape clauses in the "fine print", we know it's shady and dishonest. Why would I think God was looking to do that to me? God isn't shady. Yet many people I know and love believe just that.

I always seem to have some sort of friction with people around the same time I'm trying to find my footing on a new belief about God. Satan hopes he will be able to knock me down. He has succeeded in the past. When I want things bad enough, though, I find I need to fight with someone so that my Scotch-Irish stubbornness kicks in and I refuse to relinquish my position. Otherwise, I tend to worry too much about what people think.

The fight I needed came over the internet, on social media. While Stephanie used social media to keep everyone up to date on Samuel's medical progress, I kept quiet. I spent a lot of time surfing, watching what my friends were doing. It was a window into other people's lives, and an escape from the chaos of my own.

Just before Stephanie and I were married, Jake had pulled in a group of people on his team who had been orphaned by their line of mentorship in Amway. I kept up with a few of the others who were in that same boat on social media. One of them, who also had a day job as a street preacher, made a social media post mocking preachers who say that God wants to bless you and heal you. He was specifically targeting a preacher who had helped me understand the goodness of God, Joel Osteen.

The premise of the post to social media upset me. Not only did his mocking paint Joel in a bad light, but it also painted God in a bad light. Given his influence as a street preacher, it really concerned me. He was basically claiming that God didn't care enough to provide for the needs and desires of his people. Out of respect for this guy and Matthew 18, I confronted him on it in a private message.

I was finally overcoming this thought process myself, removing all the doubts I had about God providing for my needs, including His desire to heal. I had wrestled with this all through my twenties, and since I was now free from it, I wanted to see him set free as well.

His reply to my message was condescending and rude.

I brushed off his rudeness. I cared about this guy. I continued, pointing out a couple places where God states in the Bible that He wants to bless his children. There are many. One of those passages was the first half of Deuteronomy 28.

About Deuteronomy 28, he replied that those promises were for the Israelites that obeyed every element of the law. I continued pointing out other parts of scripture that promise the same thing, and he continued to dismiss them with the label, "They don't apply to us." As our conversation continued, I could tell by his replies that he thought he was winning the argument because he was growing even more condescending. Instead of winning his argument, I realized he wasn't really wanting to have a discussion. He wasn't wanting to reframe his thinking. I wished him well and ended the conversation.

I was left to ponder.

Because of my stubbornness, I was now more firmly convinced that God wants us to succeed, to prosper, and to be in good health. Out of sheer obstinacy, I held on to that belief. I came away ignoring even more strongly that gnawing thought that these promises weren't for me. I unfortunately had not been able to change him, but it had changed me.

As spring wore on, I realized I had missed a book Jake recommended that I should read in an earlier coaching session. My focus over the past year and a half had been on sharpening my people skills. Some books I had read multiple times over just to make sure I got those habits deep down inside of me, classics like "Bringing Out the Best in People" and "The Art of Dealing with People." They were easy reads, but more than that - the crux of my Amway business was working with people. I wanted to be highly skilled at my craft. I never left the house, or came to the hospital, without a book in my hand.

The book I missed was "Building Your Self-Image" by Josh McDowell. As the title points out, it focuses on self-image. When I finished reading "Bringing Out the Best in People," for the third time that year, and I cracked open a new copy of "Building Your Self Image." My goal in that period was to read 10 pages a day. Most self-improvement books are around 150 pages – so that put me reading in the ballpark of 20 books a year. Even with all my struggles and pursuits, I stayed consistent with my goal. I kept track of both my personal development and my business in a black 8" x 5" journal.

"Building Your Self Image" started touching on a topic that I was familiar with in principle, but I had a rough time accepting. I knew it in my head, but not in my heart. Josh shared his story of his broken home life and how God's radical love transformed him. It was difficult for me to believe God radically loved me so much that he accepted me no matter how badly I failed.

I had grown up in different churches in southern West Virginia where the focus was on living right and not sinning. The message of God's salvation was taught only to keep their hearers from going to hell. Some churches only knew preaching through fear of eternal damnation. In the entire time I attended those churches, I don't remember a single sermon that taught on how much God loves me and is good to me. I do remember constantly feeling I was falling short and displeasing God.

All my life, I felt like God didn't like me – that He just tolerated me. With this new perspective that I gained from "Building Your Self Image" - that God has a special fondness for me - I wanted to be around Him even more. I would need this revelation of how God saw me for the battles ahead.

As Josh McDowell laid out his book, I began to fully realize God viewed me in a different light than how these churches had painted. I already knew that He saw me through eyes of grace, and that He loved me gently. But Mr. McDowell led me down a path of fully seeing myself as God sees me – as accepted, as worthy, and as competent – as created in His image and a necessary part of His plan.

As Samuel was developing physically and mentally, God was developing my self-image.

The next book I read that summer was one I snagged at my spring business conference. It was called, "Ditch the Baggage, Change Your Life!" by Nancy Alcorn. For years, I had admired Nancy Alcorn's ministry, which builds, funds, and supports homes that take in abused girls and young women. While they are there, she uses her resources to teach them how to live in victory in every area of life.

I have always struggled with holding grudges against people who have wronged me, and not letting things go. While I've worked on forgiving people as Jesus calls us to do, I've still struggled with it. In Nancy's book, she lays things out with a different perspective. It helped me learn to let go of so many little hurts that I was holding. This was so important – how could I really view God as letting go of my wrongs if I struggled letting go of the wrongs of others?

By July, I had finished both books and I was beginning to see myself in a new light. I knew that God loved me, and I had let go of so many past hurts. At my summer Amway business conference, I had a chance to get in a small session with Jake and a few of his leaders. He suggested I pick up "Power Thoughts" by Joyce Meyer. "It's really helped a lot of guys on my team," he said.

I ordered it before I left, and I started it as soon as it arrived.

Joyce Meyer's book "Power Thoughts" is a sequel to one of her most famous books, "Battlefield of the Mind." In "Power Thoughts," she leads the reader through twelve different core principles of how God views you and what His desires for you are. After the first half of the book, she recommends spending the second half of the book meditating on one principle a week. There are twelve principles in the book. I started in early August and continued through the fall. I took each principle and wrote it down everywhere, I confessed it three times a day, and I made sure to re-read the chapter on that principle each evening.

Where the other books had set a good baseline for changing how I saw myself, this book took me to the next level. These confessions helped rewire my brain to see God in a new light, as a God who provides, who protects, and who loves. These three books helped me see God as a good, good Father.

During one of the few hospital visits to the hospital we made that summer, I had another interesting confrontation. It occurred in the third week of July and was an interesting parallel to my earlier fight in the spring.

All spring and summer I had worked on staying consistent with my daily routines of reading and building my business. However, any time Samuel went in the hospital, it was extremely difficult to find time to hit every daily goal.

After a few days in the hospital, I desperately wanted to hit any of my daily goals. I was leaving work for the day, and I had not accomplished anything on my list. I called Stephanie after plopping in my car, exhausted and slightly frustrated from the day and the circumstances, I asked her if she minded if I took a few minutes after work for myself.

I wanted to do some work on my business, but I couldn't push myself through the fatigue. I decided instead on grabbing a burrito at Qdoba and sitting down to read. It was at least one item covered in my daily goals.

I drove over to the local Qdoba, parked, and walked inside. After I picked up my food, I scanned the restaurant for a place to sit. The tables in the dining room were small and close together. After a glance around the room, I saw a table close to the entrance where the line to order food formed. From that seat, I could see people choosing what they wanted on their burritos. To the right and over my shoulder was the glass doored entrance. This spot afforded me a good view of the restaurant – close enough to where I could talk with someone if I wanted but separate enough in case I chose only to read.

As I sat down, I noticed a well-dressed young professional sitting at the next table. Since I was looking to expand my business with some ambitious people around my age, and this man appeared to fit my target demographic. I decided this would be a good opportunity to start a conversation with this gentleman. I barely noticed the middle-aged man who was sitting at the table across from my seat.

Arranging myself so I could eat and read, I sat my tray in front of me, offset to my left. I set my book to the right of my tray. Opening my book, "Power Thoughts", I began unwrapping my Burrito, stuffed with beef and rice and cheesy goodness. I took a bite and began to scan for where I had stopped reading. I glanced over to my left and was about to say hello to the guy my age, when the older man at the table across from me spoke up.

He nodded his head, pointed at my book, and asked, "Do you like Joyce Meyer?"

Surprised at his interest in the book, I smiled and nodded unsuspectingly while I finished chewing.

"If you are reading her books, you should probably read your Bible more," he replied, his tone dripping with disdain.

My mind jumped from trying to find rest to prepping my defense. "Here we go," I sighed. I had had many conversations like this over the years, and I had been trying to figure out how to handle these confrontations. Satan knew he had been successful at pushing me into living in fear of these authors when I was younger, so why not try again.

The older gentleman began with a spiel I heard many times before about false teachers. Predictably, he transitioned into telling me how his pastor, the pastor of another large church in Pittsburgh, was a holy man of God. He then went back to bashing Joyce Meyer, and other preachers like her. He wrapped up his soap box speech with the same conclusion with which he started: that I should read my Bible more instead of reading Joyce Meyer's books.

I've had many conversations like this. I had been analyzing the conversation from April all summer, as well as other similar conversations. I began to notice a few patterns. First, these people exhibited cult like behaviors – particularly that of worshipping their spiritual leader, exalting them above all other leaders. They would insist that their leader knew the truth, and all others were missing the mark. My second realization occurred during this conversation with the critic of Joyce Meyer.

In the past, I had tried to argue individual points, hoping I could win the arguer to the truth. A part of me had been simply trying to convince myself in those earlier discussions.

This time, I tried a different approach.

"I hear you talking down on another preacher of God's word. Have you actually read any of Joyce Meyer's books or listened to her preach?"

He dismissed my point, "No I haven't, but my Pastor has."

I continued, "What about the passages of the Bible that talk about how we are to love other Christians, or about how 'so long as the gospel is preached' it doesn't matter the motives?" I paused briefly for effect, but not long enough for him to interject, "And don't you worry about condemning a whole body of Christians whom she leads?"

This led him to pause and reflect for a moment. I briefly thought I may have had a breakthrough.

It was short lived. His moment of actual thought lasted only an instant. I could see the thought flicker across his face like a distant memory. He then waved his hand dismissively, "I'm not sure how that matters. I've heard our pastor teach on that."

I stared with my jaw hanging open slightly for a moment. How could he not see he was violating so many of God's principles and destroying the work of God with his words?

It was in that moment that I had my second deep realization - unless I was talking with his pastor, I could not change this man's mind. This man could not think for himself, and he was no more than a puppet. He had a script, and any deviation from it would cause him to shut down.

At this point, I was too angered by the belligerence of this man, who had interrupted my meal and my reading to criticize a preacher he knew nothing about, to continue our dialog. Frustrated at his arrogant and ignorant judgements, I firmly and politely ended our conversation. "You know what, I appreciate the conversation, but I think I'm done."

He stammered for a moment, once again caught off guard by my response, as he had just opened his mouth to launch into round two of his opinions.

I kept my eyes locked on his for a moment, just to make sure he knew I was done with the conversation.

He seemed to realize I was not going to be a convert for him today. Looking defeated he replied, "Um... ok. Have a good day."

Annoyed, I returned to my meal and my book. He rose awkwardly and left.

I would like to say that I recognized all of this for what it was, an attack and an attempt to keep me bound in fear. Unfortunately, I did not have a good label for this behavior at the time, and I spent the better part of a week pondering the conversation.

It's unfortunate that Christians attack other Christians. Had he any idea what I was going through, he may have kept his mouth shut – or maybe he would have been more vocal.

In the end, I needed that pressure to help me realize I was on the right path. The Holy Spirit was using these books I was reading to teach me about my self-image, and that I needed to be strong to stand against the opinions of people who were wrong in their interpretation of the Bible. I needed to have that strength of conviction in myself to be able to stand in faith on the principles that God was about to teach me. I needed to be able to stand against the opinions of other people in general.

I was still upset about and processing that verbal altercation a few days later when a gentleman in the Hospital cafeteria asked me about the same book. "Do you like that book?" he asked.

I froze, recoiling slightly. The book sat on my tray, along with the food I was choosing – a cheeseburger and sushi. The similarity to the previous question in Qdoba, coupled with the remaining sting of judgement from that conversation, left me on edge.

After a moment, I caught myself. I realized I couldn't assume that this man was going to react the same as the man in Qdoba. I stiffened my spine, looked him in the eye, and replied, "Yes, I really like the book. It's helping me out a lot."

"Hmm," he said pensively, "I'll have to check that out then. I had a friend recommend it to me."

Realizing this wouldn't be a hostile conversation, I relaxed. "Yeah, I would definitely recommend it."

I gave him a smile and we each went on our way.

CHAPTER 7

ONE

"For no matter how many promises God has made, they are 'Yes' in Christ." ~ 2 Cor 1:20 NIV

I typically find a baby's first birthday a waste of time, but something our Pastor's wife Kate said to me struck me as wise.

Early in the month of September, Kate, Stephanie, and I were talking in the parking lot after church. Kate is fantastic at caring for people who are going through tough seasons, always with a huge smile and an encouraging word.

After briefly catching up, Stephanie pulled an invitation out of her purse for Samuel's first birthday party. "We'd love it if you guys could join," Steph said, handing her the full sheet flyer she had made and had printed.

Kate nodded and took the invitation, staring down and reading it, her brow slightly furrowed. "We'll see if we can make it," she said with a smile, but the look on her face said that she doubted if she could. She was no doubt thinking over the multiple things on their family's schedule. At the time, they not only had the activities of 4 kids to keep up with, but she was the worship pastor and her husband, Chris, was the campus pastor for our church of thousands of people.

Knowing their schedule must be full, I attempted to relieve any pressure. "It's no big deal if you can't come," I said, making sure to give a genuine smile. "I know you guys have a lot on your plate."

Kate paused, and then gave us a big smile and said, "No, this is important to celebrate. You guys have gone through a lot, and Samuel has endured a lot. It's important to celebrate making it to a year."

That struck me. We nodded and said our goodbyes, and I left thinking over what Kate said. I knew I wanted to celebrate Samuel's first birthday, but I felt guilty for asking people to come. Many of my friends are active in building businesses and have a lot of important things they are working towards, life changing things. On top of that, Samuel would never remember his first birthday. I also felt guilty for taking away from my own productivity. I was still very much working to build my business. Between the planning and the party, I would lose at least one week of productivity, if not two.

Kate was right, though. We had fought hard to get this far. On top of that, many people were praying and standing in faith for Samuel's healing. If Samuel had been born when I was born, in the 80's, they wouldn't have been able to do anything for him medically. Samuel had already had 3 successful heart surgeries, and he was growing steadily. This was worth celebrating. We invited everyone, and many people wanted to be involved.

Stephanie and I had originally scheduled Samuel's birthday party for the weekend before his actual birthday. Unfortunately, Samuel had to go back into the hospital for SVT two weeks before his birthday. It had been almost two months since we had been back to Children's.

As the day drew close, it looked like Samuel would be getting out of the hospital one day before the party. We didn't want to have that type of pressure of preparing for a large gathering having just come home from the hospital. We had invited well over 50 people, after all.

We chose to postpone the celebration for the following weekend and to just do a smaller event. Less people were able to come, but it's a memory I treasure to this day. It was another reminder to me of the necessity in celebrating the victories we have, even if we haven't finished fully achieved our goal.

The time Samuel had spent in the hospital, adjusting medications and healing from operations, had stunted a lot of his physical development. For those unfamiliar with how children progress: a typical child starts to crawl at six months. At around a year, a child starts walking and talking. Samuel still wasn't crawling by his first birthday.

It was then that the thought popped in my head that Samuel might not make it to an age when he could walk. I knew exactly what that was - fear. Fear has this way of conjuring up the worst-case scenarios in your head. It's amazing that Satan knows how much power your imagination has; he uses it all the time to pull people down.

I put that thought from my head and began to confess that Samuel would walk, and I joined it with my confession that he would live long in the land and grow strong in the land. Soon after, God backed up my confession with a vision. I don't remember when exactly God gave it to me. I just remember seeing this scene in my head, almost as if someone had spliced it into my mental pictures when I wasn't looking.

In the vision, I saw Samuel running barefoot around our back yard. I could see his little toddler legs carrying him around on the green grass as he laughed. His dark blue onesie contrasted his pale skin and blonde hair. He had a sippy cup curled in his left arm, holding it close to him so he wouldn't drop it, the snaps of his onesie hanging loose at his crotch.

After this vision appeared in my memory, I held tight to it. I carried it around as a mental token reminding me that Samuel would be well. When I needed a visual reminder of God's promises, I pulled this image up and declared His promises all the louder. I knew for this to happen, Samuel had to make it through.

The month after Samuel's first birthday, in early October, he finally began crawling. We celebrated the victory and were thankful he finally hit that milestone.

Unfortunately, this small victory turned into another hospital visit a few weeks later.

I had just pulled in our driveway after getting home from work one evening. My car in park but still running when Stephanie rang my phone. Surprised she hadn't seen me pull in from the kitchen window, I answered and was about to tell her I was home. I got out the word, "Hey," before she interrupted, sobbing hysterically into the phone, and saying something about Samuel falling.

I paused, sitting in my car with one leg out the open door as she tried to frantically relay what had just happened.

"Samuel fell down the stairs," I finally made out between her wails.

"I'm outside," I said and darted into the house, sprinting through the garage, and making my way to the bottom of the stairs in our duplex.

Stephanie sat on the second stair from the bottom, clutching Samuel to her and sobbing. She clutched him tight to her, his body lying flat on her lap.

As I drew closer, I was surprised to see he was staring at me, smiling that I was finally home.

I pried him away from her enough to look him over. While he seemed slightly scared at how much Mommy was crying, he was unphased by what had just happened – unaware that he had just tumbled down thirteen stairs.

I took off his onesie and checked for bruises or any other injuries, while simultaneously trying to calm my wife with my words. I saw no red marks or bruising, and no where I touched seemed to hurt him. As Stephanie saw that he seemed fine, she began to calm down and started to relate the full story to me.

She had just arrived home from picking up Samuel and some groceries. She strapped him in his highchair to eat dinner while she started making dinner for the both of us. When Samuel finished, he decided it would be funny to throw his food on the ground. When mommy reprimanded him, he laughed at her, excited to see her riled. Having enough of his orneriness, Stephanie took him out of the highchair, wiped off his hands, and put him on the floor to crawl around. She couldn't see the open door to the basement from where she stood, and she forgot that she had not closed it.

Samuel crawled off of the hardwood floors of our kitchen and into the carpeted hallway while Stephanie went back to making dinner. After a few short moments of peace, Stephanie heard a series of loud thuds coming from the stairs. Realizing what happened, she bolted to the basement door and down the stairs.

There were 13 carpeted steps in our house (at one point, to get fit, I was climbing our stairs multiple times a day, so I knew how many we had). He had tumbled down all of them and came to rest on the carpeted landing without a scratch or a red mark. We were amazed that he had not hit one of the poles or tumbled off the side of the stairs.

Realizing this, I immediately praised God. I had been confessing that God protects my child because Samuel (and Izaiah) are children of the righteous. I knew that God had protected him.

We returned to the kitchen carrying Samuel, making sure to shut the door this time. We discussed whether we should take him to the hospital out of precaution. As Stephanie made phone calls to chat with the doctors and get their opinion, the Holy Spirit reminded me of Psalm 91. It says that God's angels "will hold up your feet, lest you strike a stone." I had a tendency to attribute this passage as being solely about Jesus, as it is quoted in the gospel by Jesus, who is referring to himself. While Jesus falls under that promise, it is actually written about the author, which is Moses according to Jewish tradition.

While Samuel looked and acted perfectly fine, we still took him the hospital to confirm he was ok. The Doctors ran multiple tests on him, but everything came back perfect. He didn't even have a red mark on him.

One test, however, did not come back perfect. The excitement from falling down our stairs must have triggered his SVT. We still ended up having to stay in the hospital for a couple of days while they attempted to adjust his medication.

Up until March of that year, I had been pushing heavily forward with my Amway business. All through Stephanie's pregnancy and up through Samuel's first few surgeries, I continued to prospect and work at finding the right people to fill the roles I needed. The back-to-back surgeries in March and April had left me so beaten that I needed recovery. The spring and summer brought much needed rest in every area. While I had not stopped working on myself and my business, I had slowed in seeking out partners to expand. It seemed every single time I tried to move forward; Samuel would end up in the hospital. If that didn't slow me down, then a hospital visit would turn into a surgery.

As my own heart healed and summer wore on, I began to wonder how I could stay consistent in building my business in the face of Samuel's medical issues. I asked Jake about it, and he suggested I dig into Kenneth Copeland's and Frederick Price's teachings, especially those on confession. On Jake's suggestion, I picked up the cd set for "The Authority of the Believer" by Copeland and "The Power of Positive Confession" by Frederick C. Price.

I dug heavily into both. My total commute time to and from work was an hour and a half. I also was driving once a week to Morgantown, which is a 3-hour round trip. I had plenty of time to listen.

The boldness of Kenneth Copeland was new to me, and it was somewhat off putting. I often found myself questioning his interpretations of scriptures. His points challenged so many of the things I had been taught in church and so many of the conclusions

I had come to believe about God. Yet every time I went back and read the scripture he referenced, and prayed over the interpretation, I found that Copeland was right.

Throughout my twenties, my interpretation of scripture was shaped by a couple of things. First, the leaders in Amway would teach from a conference or on a CD how to stand on God's promises. I would then read those promises and find more of my own. I would get excited about those promises and start to accept them as God wanting them for me. Then I would hang out with other Christians and leaders in my church or another church, and they would say something along the lines of, "Yeah, I know that's in there, BUT …." They would proceed to explain away God's promises with their own experiences. Often, they would point out why they didn't think God meant what the Bible was so clearly stating.

These local Christians left me incredibly confused. I was close to them, and I would back off from my confessions and question my convictions. Other Christians in the same circles would use labels - "prosperity gospel" and "false teachers" were the most common. Their boldness in teaching left me afraid of the teachers who taught differently than the preachers we sat under. You should take warning that if fear is shaping your decisions and beliefs, you should question what you have decided to believe. Also, if someone causes you to doubt the goodness of God, you might consider avoiding that person. When I sat under these teachers, I could only come up with one core conclusion: God is not a good and trustworthy god.

I am deeply thankful for my Amway team. Were it not for their leaders, I would have no one challenging these misconceptions. Jake's suggestion that I should listen to Kenneth Copeland was exactly what I needed to step forward boldly.

If I could sum up Copeland's entire body of preaching in two sentences, it would be this: if God has made a promise in the Bible, then God means exactly what He said. Kenneth Copeland is going to believe that promise no matter what he sees or hears or thinks, laying claim to the promises in the Bible just as they are written.

Eventually my thinking and beliefs shifted as I listened to what Copeland said. I dug deeper into the Bible to see these promises for myself and spent time seeking the Lord's presence every day. The more I listened and studied, the more my hesitations about his teachings went away.

It was in this same period that I heard two local preachers give two messages that established for me a firm footing. John Nuzzo of Victory Family Church shared his testimony of how his son was healed of severe autism at 5 years old, by standing on his confession of faith. The one passage that stuck out the most was how he taught about Romans 3:4 (NIV), which states "…Let God be true, and human being a liar…" Before he began, he addressed the elephant in the room when it comes to healing. Pastor Nuzzo said it this way (paraphrased), "I don't want to ignore people who've lost loved ones or haven't seen healing, but I just had to choose that God's word was true and everyone else was a liar." Pastor Nuzzo was echoing the same sentiment as Kenneth Copeland – that God's promises are trustworthy, even when someone else's circumstances seem to indicate that they aren't. Through Nuzzo's example, I found the courage to trust God's promises for Samuel.

The other preacher who made an impact on me was the preacher at my church, Jeff Leake. We were sitting in church at the main

Hampton location one Sunday when he called out a scripture that hit me in the core of my soul. As he was walking through his message, he shared 2 Corinthians 1:20 (NIV), which states "For no matter how many promises God has made, they are 'Yes' in Christ." He went on to teach how this is exactly as it reads – if God made a promise anywhere in the Bible, then they are ours because of Christ's sacrifice.

All summer long I had had this nagging feeling in the back of my head that I was missing some detail in God's promises. I was afraid that I was going to offend God by relying on Him to fulfill a promise that was intended for someone else. Worse, I was afraid that God would not fulfill the promise because I didn't qualify – as I'm not a Jew, and I surely don't follow every detail of the Jewish law. This verse in 2 Corinthians annihilated those thoughts. Because of what Jesus did for me, there wasn't a promise in the Bible for which I couldn't lay claim. This was a game changer.

It's important to understand God's character – He says He is good. Now, I no longer had to rely solely on God's goodness to believe that Samuel would be healthy and whole. I had now found it in His Word that what I was believing was for me and was true. The Bible can't be half true – either God is a good Father, or the entire Bible is a lie.

CHAPTER 8

THANKSGIVING

"Life isn't about waiting for the storms to pass.... It's about learning to dance in the rain." ~ Vivian Greene

The doctors told us Samuel might outgrow the SVT and his heart would no longer race. Given how infrequently we had visited the hospital since April, we were beginning to hope that that might be the case. Instead, Samuel's growth was causing his medications doses to not work appropriately.

On Tuesday evening, November 10th, we once again found Samuel in SVT at bedtime and drove him to the ER at Children's. After the usual attempts to stop his SVT in the ER, they admitted Samuel and we settled in for the night, still in SVT.

From September to December is my busy season at work. On top of the workload, I also had run out of vacation and sick time. I was desperately trying to stretch every minute of paid leave I could. While we could afford for Stephanie to miss a week or two, for me to take time off would've made it incredibly difficult to keep our bills paid. After we took Samuel to the hospital on the night of the 10th, I went in to work late the next morning.

Samuel spent the entire week in SVT. Even while sleeping, his heart rate never dropped below 160 beats per minute. Dr. Arora had spent the last 14 months trying to keep Samuel's heart rate in check. The mechanical valve and the risk of clotting again put extra pressure on Dr. Arora to keep his heart rate within a child's normal range.

When the heart is functioning normally, it keeps blood flowing through the body. When the heart is in SVT, which is pretty much the maximum rate a heart can beat, the structures of the heart can't keep blood flowing well. The blood begins to pool around the heart valve, and blood that isn't in motion tends to clot. Clotting inevitably leads to the valve not opening and closing properly, with the added possibility of more damage like the strokes we had seen in April.

After a weak of Samuel's heart beating at the maximum rate, Dr. Arora felt it prudent to make sure the heart valve was still holding up well. He put in the orders for an echo, and eventually a tech came to run the test. Stephanie was at the hospital with Samuel, and I was working when Dr. Arora made the decision. When the echo was finished, Stephanie called me on my work phone to fill me in on how it went.

When my desk phone rang, I glanced down from my computer screens to see who was calling. Certain people in my office tended to be pushy and occasionally I would get calls from recruiters with job offers – I didn't want to talk to either of those categories of people. Seeing it was Steph, I eagerly snatched the phone.

"Hey babe," I said with a smile. I was always excited to hear from my wife.

She jumped right in, "So Dr. Arora ordered an echo. The tech just left."

"Did she say anything?" I asked, a bit surprised by the news. My spreadsheets and database queries vanished from my mind. I spun my office chair around to face the fake wood bookshelf with a mahogany stain, staring at the trinkets I had placed on the top shelf and the grey wall behind it, which was covered with an oversized map of the company's wells.

"Well, she told me that she can't officially interpret the results, but she's pretty sure the valve's not working right."

I inhaled involuntarily, "Hmm."

We chatted for a few more minutes before I returned to my work.

Later that afternoon, Steph called me back. Dr. Arora confirmed our concerns: Samuel's heart valve had a clot. One of the leaflets of the artificial heart valve was stuck open, causing it to malfunction.

Despite imminent surgery, we had to wait a full day before a room became available, as the CICU was full. When we finally got Samuel in a room, they booked surgery for the following morning.

It had been seven months since Samuel's last surgery. He was so much larger now. After some measurements, the surgical team estimated he would be able to put a valve in that was two sizes larger than the current valve.

Dr. Arora explained to us the importance of this in his morning rounds, "A larger valve may enable us to wait longer before we would have to replace it again. If all works as expected, he might go until he's a teenager before he needs another replacement."

Since Samuel was now over a year old, Dr. Arora brought up another option to combat Samuel's SVT, a process called an Ablation. An Ablation is where the Surgeon will selectively kill some of the extra nerves that cause the heart to short-circuit. They typically do this by cauterizing some of the errant nerves on the exterior of the heart. This cuts out the duplicate pathways and is a common procedure in adult patients to stop SVT. We felt this was a good move, so they chose to perform an ablation on Samuel in addition to the valve replacement surgery. If this were to work, this could be the last surgery and hospital stay Samuel would have for years – until his heart valve was too small or simply wore out. If both surgeries were successful, Samuel might be a teen again before he would need another surgery.

As we made mental preparations for another surgery, I questioned the timing. Why was this happening now? I was finally starting to feel like I could return to a normal life, where I could move forward in having a normal marriage and being a normal Dad and fully pursuing my Amway business on top of my job. I knew that we were waging war against Satan and his armies, and that God was on our side. But what I couldn't understand was why now, just as I was emotionally healing and moving forward. Why was God allowing this battle for Samuel's health to capsize my life once again? Since I was still being mentored by Jake, I shot him a text and asked him the hard question on my mind. "Jake, why does Samuel go back in for a surgery or into the hospital every time I try to start moving forward with my business?"

His reply wasn't philosophical.

"I don't know, R.L." he texted back.

I was still frustrated with the situation, but his reply comforted me. I often feared I was missing some intricate detail, or I wasn't doing something I should be doing. Jake had waged many more spiritual battles than I. Since he had no advice, I took comfort in knowing that I was doing everything I could do.

With my concerns settled on whether I was spiritually prepared, I turned my attention to my job. Samuel's surgery was exactly one week before Thanksgiving, on Thursday the 19th. There was a major deadline for our company's yearend process the day after Samuel's surgery, on the 20th. Our entire department was responsible for preparing this submission. I was the lowest ranking employee in our department, despite having more seniority than anyone other than our manager. In years past I had volunteered to take over the majority of the work, hoping for an eventual promotion. Instead, I was left doing the work while the rest of the team avoided the process for all but a few items. This year was no different, and I was left to take care of the process alone. I stayed late at work that Tuesday evening, hoping to get all that I could finished before I took of work on Thursday.

That next day, I worked with laser focus. Even though I skipped lunch, I still barely managed to finish my tasks by the end of the day. I was elated when I finished all that was needed, ahead of schedule; but at the same time, I was exhausted from having done so much work so quickly.

After I emailed the documents needed for submission, I packed up my bag and rushed to my car. I quickly made the way out of my work's office complex and on to I-376 East. Traffic moved swiftly as I made my way off the exit, only to stop a mile further down the road. Rush hour traffic going into the city in the evenings always moved in this fashion. It runs at normal speeds until it reaches one of many bottle necks, causing traffic to come to a complete stop. I eventually made it to, and then through the Fort Pitt tunnel, and made my way out of it onto the mess of intersections and bridges that flow through the edge of downtown and over the three rivers below. As I exited the tunnel, my emotional fortitude began to crack. The exhaustion from the hospital stays, my workload, the unfairness of my work environment, and the worries about my life broke through everything that was holding me together. The wall keeping my emotions in check imploded.

By the time I pulled down the ramp to merge onto Route 28, I was sobbing so bad I could barely see the cars in front of me. Heading north towards the hospital, I struggled through tears and with the emotional release as my entire chest convulsed withs sobs. There was no place to pull off the road until I gained my composure. My emotions demanded to be dealt with immediately, so I continued driving.

As I continued up 28, the questions came slowly from the depths of my soul:

"God, where are you?"

"Why have you not yet healed Samuel?"

"Why are we having another surgery? I thought this was done."

Over the last two days as we waited for a bed and then for surgery, Samuel's health had deteriorated rapidly due to his mitral valve not working properly. He had been crawling and happy most of the week. Now he was laboring just to breathe, unable to even lift his head off his bed.

As I saw the sign for the hospital exit, which was on the left, the thought occurred that I should choose to worship God in my pain. It didn't feel natural for me to do so, but I did it anyway.

I turned on the car stereo of my old Acura and switched the CD player to Hillsong's Zion album. I could barely see the controls through my tears. I blinked heavily to clear my vision so I could make out the skip button, trying to keep focused on the road and the traffic around me. I eventually found it, and skipped to track 7, "Love is War." Pushing through the sobs, I began to sing and to worship out of my pain and desperation. It was exhausting to sing. The fatigue hung heavy like a wet sweater in the winter, and the fear for Samuel's life resonated at my core. I continued to sing God's praise anyway. As I continued singing, it became easier.

The song "Love is War" ended as I was coming up the ramp off of the exit, and "Nothing Like Your Love" began to play. I continued singing this second song as I made a right at the stoplight at the top and onto the 40th street bridge. Traffic across the bridge was backed up and slow, which gave me plenty of time to sing through the tears. As I sat awaiting my turn to move forward one more car length, I stared down the river at the orange sun casting its long evening rays into my passenger window.

I reached the bridge of the song at the same time I reached the crest of the arched bridge. The bridge on this song repeats over and over, declaring God's goodness. The more I sang, the more determined I was to continue to do so with every ounce of my remaining strength. As I sang, I thought of how God's promises were the only truth I chose to know. When the bridge ended, I rewound to the beginning of the bridge and started again.

As I approached the end of the bridge and turned down a side street that I used as a shortcut, not only had the heaviness all but dissipated, but my strength was beginning to return. My change of focus and the presence of God, which was ushered in by my worship, was giving me strength. I still felt emotionally raw, but I no longer felt empty. In tearful defiance, as I made my way through the brick rowhouses down the blacktop side streets, I restarted the section of the bridge one more time and sang the lyrics at the top of my lungs.

As I sing, my heart cried out, "The Devil would not have his way with the death of my son." I sang through the tears to my God, to boldly declare in the face of these bleak circumstances that He would not fail on His promises. I sang to boldly declare, in Satan's face, that God was on my side and that my son would live. I sang to declare that no matter how it looks, my God wins!

"Your love's amazing it fills my heart and I cry out,
there is none like You,
there is nothing like your love...."

By the time I reached the top of the hill and the parking garage, all but the lightest dredges of heaviness were gone.

I made my way into the hospital, carrying my bags and still humming the tune. I checked in at the front desk and headed up to the 7th floor. Samuel, who was now sleeping most of the time, was sleeping when I entered his room. Stephanie and I were exhausted as well, and so we fell asleep at 8 P.M. that night.

I awoke that night at 12:30.

I laid on the pullout cushions that pulled out from underneath the futon where Stephanie laid sleeping. I grabbed my phone and started scrolling through social media, hoping I would fall back to sleep. The room was dark, illuminated by the lights from Samuel's heart monitor and IV, and the light underneath the door.

I eventually gave up and made my way down the hall to the corner sitting area. Our unit, 7A, was known as the heart wing. It was set up in a large square with rooms on the exterior walls. The nurse's stations were on the inside corners, and storage was on the interior walls. Each outside corner of the wing had something unique: Two corners had short hallways that led to windows. Another corner of the wing was the exit. The Southwest corner of the unit had a small sitting area, where I was now seated. It was carpeted with rough, dark grey carpet tiles, unlike the hallways which were a beige linoleum. Two walls of the sitting area were lined with floor to ceiling windows that looked out onto Lawrenceville and the hillside up to Polish Hill. In the distance, to the west, I could just make out the tops of the buildings of downtown Pittsburgh.

This area was quiet. The view of the city lights gave a gentle beauty compared to the tension in the depths of my soul. It had been so long since I had fought ... since we had fought for Samuel's life. The accuser of our souls, the devil himself, was desperately trying to trick us into accepting any doubt. Like someone desperate to hand out flyers, at every turn he was hoping to give us a doubt to carry with us.

I sat with my journal on my lap, pouring out my heart through my pen. I wrote of the events of the day, and I reminded myself of the perspective that I had come to know in Samuel's first set of surgeries: that God was on my side and wanted Samuel healthy and whole. Satan stood on the opposite side. Both offered me a choice of faith – faith in death, or faith in God's word, which was life. I refused to even give words to the death that Satan was trying so desperately to get me to take.

After I emptied my thoughts and emotions, I finished by filling my mind with God's word. I turned to Psalm 112. It was my habit in my morning reading to copy each verse that resonated with me into my journal. As I sat there in the middle of the night, I slowly copied each line into my journal. With each sentence, my mind settled on God's words spoken through the psalmist – focusing both on the promises and the praises. Each line slowly relieved the pressure as my soul clung to my heavenly Father. I finished close to 3:00 A.M. Relieved, I packed up my journal and made my way back to the room and fell asleep.

The next morning, Samuel was taken down to surgery in the same fashion as the last four surgeries. He came through surgery as expected, and the doctor was able to replace his heart valve. This time the doctor performed an ablation as well. Excitingly, although he went into surgery in SVT, the ablation appeared to have worked. His heart was beating in a normal rhythm when we saw him in recovery. We were cautiously hopeful that this might be the "one."

The day after Samuel's surgery, I was back at work as though nothing had happened. That Sunday, Stephanie and I celebrated our second wedding anniversary. Since Samuel was still recovering from surgery and sleeping quite a bit, we managed to slip across the street and grab dinner from an Indian restaurant across from Children's Hospital. We celebrated two years of marriage over Chicken Tikka Masala, rice, and Naan. The restaurant was very tastefully decorated, with beige walls and dark wood tables and floors. The décor mixed modern and classy in a unique way. Despite the circumstances, we were able to have an almost normal celebration.

I worked the three days before Thanksgiving, unlike years prior, because I didn't have the vacation time to take it off. I was now saving every day just in case we had another emergency. After finishing work at 5 PM that Wednesday evening, I drove down to Washington, PA to meet Izaiah's mom, Christina. Izaiah would be staying with us from Wednesday until Saturday, since that Sunday was Christina's birthday. We met at the Krispy Kreme donut shop for the exchange because it was in an area we could get into and out of without traffic. As a bonus, it also had donuts, coffee, and clean restrooms.

Christina and I briefly chatted about Izaiah's week. I eventually packed him into the car, and we headed back North towards Pittsburgh. Rather than heading home, we drove through the city and straight to the hospital. I parked in the mid-campus garage and we both made our way down the long hallway that goes from the garage to the main lobby of the hospital. When heading into the hospital from the mid-campus garage, the right side the of hallway has a long mural that covers the entire length. This mural has patterned shapes and animals that morph from one pattern to the next – butterflies that morph into flowers that morph into kittens, and on down the hall in a rainbow shade. The left side of the hallway is line with support pillars every 30 feet that support the outside wall of the hospital, with white painted drywall running 8 feet high to a short row of windows stretching the entire length. Izaiah, a couple months shy of 6 years old, was always enthralled at the murals and the designs in the tiles on the floor. We were not in a hurry, since Samuel was still sedated from the surgery, and so we slowly made our way down the hallway.

We eventually made it to the end of the hallway, where there is a gift shop and then a pharmacy. We turned right into the main lobby where the overhanging roof opened to two story ceilings. To the left was a small waiting area with no walls, adorned with funky magenta couches and touch screen devices to entertain the kids. Past the magenta couches with no backs were two story windows, which showed a 3-lane covered drop off area. It was lit with orangish lights, as it was currently nighttime.

In this portion of the lobby with the funky magenta couches, the ceiling hung low and was covered with wood, punctuated with evenly spaced recessed lighting. Izaiah was always fascinated by the touch screens, and it was always a struggle to get him to not run directly to the games to play when he saw them. Since it was the first day of my Thanksgiving break and we would be heading to the much less kid friendly CICU, I let him play for a few moments before calling him over to get checked in.

After this part of the lobby, the ceiling opened to the full two stories. Hanging from the ceiling, suspended by cables, were various rods – most likely an artistic rendering of something. I never figured out what it was meant to represent. To the right, at first, was a hallway and the restroom, then a long section of desks under the open area with 4 different stations and computers. The first desk was set back against the wall and had a digital readout to show the amount you would pay on for parking. The other three stations sat forward 10 feet into the main lobby and were all part of one long desk. The edges were roped off to lead people to form lines. Every day when we entered the hospital, we had to check in at these desks, giving our I.D., Samuel's name, and his patient number. The attendants gave us a sticker with our name and the date of check-in, as well as an access card to Samuel's floor.

After checking in, we made our way past the desks towards the elevators on the same wall. We passed by a security guard who sat at a podium just in front of the elevators who made sure everyone had their pink sticker marking the current date. I had Izaiah push the button to the fourth floor. He was accustomed to pushing the seven, but I told him that Samuel was on a different floor because he had just had surgery. Izaiah softly said, "Oh," and pressed the black circle with a white four in the center.

The elevator took us to the fourth floor, and we wove our way past the surgical waiting room. Izaiah and I took our time as we traversed the speckled floors, beside the purple walls, into the waiting area for the CICU. After we made our way through the waiting room, we reached the check-in desk for the CICU. Judy was working that night, as she was most nights during the week. She was one of the ladies who worked that desk, and she always had a smile for us. She checked us in a second time, gushing over Izaiah as made our way to the entrance. The CICU is laid out like a blocky "C", and we eventually reached the middle section of the "C" where Samuel's room was situated.

Stephanie and I chatted for a few moments after Izaiah and I said hello. She discussed Samuel's medical updates with me, and I caught her up with updates on Christina and Izaiah. Stephanie and I were both exhausted, but peaceful. The conversation wasn't long.

As soon as we settled in, we heard a knock at the door. A brown-haired woman in her twenties, dressed in street clothes, was standing outside Samuel's room.

"Would you like me to play music for you?" she asked as I held the door open.

I was curious and a little bewildered. "What do you play?" I replied.

"I play the harp," she said, pointing her hand behind her. Somehow, I had missed the large wooden harp that sat beside her in the CICU hallway.

This was all a bit surreal, as I had never seen a harp in person, much less heard one played. After I processed the momentary shock, I was excited for the distraction. I figured it would be good for the boys. I turned to Stephanie, "Babe, what do you think?"

"Sure," she replied.

I've played a few different musical instruments since I was 12 years old, so I was excited to see such a rare instrument. It was much larger than I expected a harp to be. When she sat down to play, the harp was taller than her. The strings were colored different primary colors to represent different notes. As she adjusted herself to start playing, I asked her a few technical questions about the instrument. My experiences with the harp up until now were limited to 'Bugs Bunny" cartoons.

After my questions came Izaiah's fascination. I could tell he was excited, but he kept quiet, taking it in visually.

When she was fully settled, she returned a question to us, "Are there any songs you guys would like to hear?"

Stephanie and I looked at each other, and she answered, "I can't think of anything."

I shook my head, indicating a no.

She turned to Izaiah, "Are there any songs you would like to hear?"

He mentioned a song he knew from school that she didn't recognize. She replied with a song she knew, but he didn't recognize the one she mentioned. It took a few tries to find something they both knew. Finally, she settled on the alphabet song.

Video: Izaiah and the Harp
http://www.rlshawver.com/ftcihp-vid2

As she began to play, I pulled out my phone to video.

"How did you know how to play that?!" Izaiah asked amazed, shocked that she was able to play a song he recognized. I adored the simplicity of his question and the way he said it.

She was focused on playing her instrument and couldn't answer. Instead, she simply nodded and kept gently plucking the notes.

Izaiah began to sing the song with her, "A – B – C – D – E -F – G." He was mesmerized by her playing a song he knew so well.

As Izaiah continued, the alarm on Samuel's heart monitor began to go off, ringing like someone's phone. It rang through the last few bars of her playing, neither she nor Izaiah realizing the gravity of the beeps. Stephanie and I looked at the monitor and then at each other. The sinking feeling – after seeing his heart rate at double speed, of knowing he was in SVT, overwhelmed us both.

Our hopes of this ordeal being over were dashed as the monitor chimed, mocking our hope. Samuel only stayed out of SVT for less than a full week after the ablation. Stephanie pressed the nurse call button.

As the harpist and Izaiah were finishing their duet, a team of doctors and nurses rushed into Samuel's room, indicating that they must have seen it on the monitors outside. The young harpist, realizing quickly she would be in the way, excused herself and her harp out of the room and moved on to the next patient. The mass of nurses, doctors, and hospital equipment made the room incredibly tight. I knew there was nothing I could do, and most likely Izaiah and I were in the way. Also, I really didn't want to be there. I had hoped this was the end of our journey and that Samuel could proceed with life as a normal child.

I turned to Stephanie, "I'm going to take Izaiah downstairs to get some food."

She nodded in reply, her face showing anger at the situation. She barely looked up from what the doctors and nurses were doing to get Samuel's heart rate under control. I couldn't get close enough to kiss her, so I told her, "I love you," and led Izaiah down to the cafeteria.

When we arrived, I chose a tray and we walked through the various lines, grabbing the items we wanted for dinner. I paid, and we chose to sit in the comfortable leather chairs set against the front wall, away from the tables and hard plastic chairs in the rest of the cafeteria.

As he and I settled in and started eating our food, I turned my attention to Izaiah and away from my thoughts. Stephanie and I were well seasoned with the health struggles and emergency situations, but Izaiah had only caught it in small doses. "Izaiah, what did you think of all that up there?"

Video: Izaiah being goofy
http://www.rlshawver.com/ftcihp-vid3

He shrugged his shoulders, jutted out his chin, and jerked his head to the left, then to the right, then back to the left again. He grinned from ear to ear as he did so, and he had that look in his eyes of being ornery and goofy. He continued this a few times in the same weird manner. He was trying to make me laugh, and he succeeded.

I lost it at this point. The laughter felt good. Izaiah giggled heartily at being able to make me guffaw so loudly. His head shake gesture reminded me of my younger brother Mike; it was something he would do. I made Izaiah let me record it to send it to Mike.

With the stress of Samuel's situation forgotten, Izaiah and I talked over dinner about his time in kindergarten. When we finished with the food and conversation, we returned to Samuel's room on the fourth floor.

Stephanie was exhausted. I checked to see if she needed anything for the night before I left or for the next day when I returned. She gave me one or two items to grab, as she always did. After that, I said a prayer over Samuel, kissed them both, and took Izaiah home for the evening.

The next morning, we celebrated Thanksgiving in the hospital. Despite Samuel's episode of SVT, the doctor's released him out of the CICU and back to 7A.

While there are games, toys, game rooms, and even an area to drop off your kids for a few hours, there aren't a lot of healthy kids around the hospital in these areas for another healthy kid to play. When Izaiah was with us, it was sometimes difficult to keep him entertained. He wanted interaction and companionship, and our stress didn't make good company for a 5-year-old. That morning, I had an idea for a fun activity.

A few weekends prior, when we were at home, our good friends Dane and Karen showed us a video called Gymkhana. In the video, a driver drifts his tuned car all over a closed course in various cities with incredible precision. There are multiple cameras recording, and it was exciting to watch.

Since Izaiah was still small enough to fit in the cars that toddlers sit in - the red ones with the yellow top, I had a great idea. He often would climb in the car, and I would take him "drifting" around the hospital. We had done this several times and Izaiah never seemed to want to stop. I figured to make it entertaining, we should video it – Gymkhana style.

I strapped Stephanie's phone to the car with a few twist ties I found, and we proceeded to drift up and down the hallways, into the elevators, and onto as many floors as we could without being too obnoxious. We rode the elevator down and drifted though the cafeteria on the 4th floor. Then we rode back up and drifted through two wings of the 7th floor. We rode back down to the 6th floor where there is a large open area and a small outdoor terrace. Reaching the end of my energy, we rode back up to 7A. I upload the video to YouTube. It's not worth sharing here, but it still made for a great memory.

In the afternoon, the hospital staff notified us that there was a special meal being catered for us on the 4th floor. A couple whose child had been in the hospital catered a very nice Thanksgiving dinner for the families stuck in the

Video: Playing the Wii
http://www.rlshawver.com/ftcihp-vid4

hospital over the holiday. They were even kind enough to help serve the food, and they were as kind in person.

That evening, Samuel fell asleep early, as he was still recovering from the surgery. My brother, Mike, had come to visit us. The four of us - Stephanie, Izaiah, Mike, and I - decided the playroom in 7A was the best way to spend Thanksgiving evening. We sat on bean bags and played Wii Bowling. Izaiah got a huge laugh when you threw the ball the wrong way and the Wii characters jumped.

The next few days, as Samuel was getting stronger, I was able to take him out into the hospital in a new gadget. Since our little man still wasn't walking, my mom bought him a baby walker – the type you set the baby in. There's a tray for their things, and wheels on the bottom. We debated whether to use it; Canada had banned these toys and there were multiple websites cautioning parents to stay away from them. There was a lot of loose scientific sounding claims about how these affected the baby's development, but the one legitimate concern was that babies might try to take the stairs in them. Largely, I find that the baby toy industry warnings can be geared towards the absolute worst of society. In our circumstances, we wouldn't be letting him run unattended, and there were no stairs for him to attempt to climb in the hospital.

While I felt there was no problem in letting Samuel use it, the trend of shaming and even bringing legal action against unwitting parents put me on edge. I was concerned with what the hospital staff thought, as I didn't want Child Protective Services showing up at the hospital to accuse us of abusing our child. I never know when a nosy parent or doctor might feel like reporting me for using a "dangerous" toy. This may have been my overactive imagination, but the last thing I wanted was another battle I didn't need to fight.

I spoke with a doctor who was familiar about Samuel's situation. She actually debated the merits of using it with herself out loud. After a few moments, she came to the same conclusion as I had. Given that Samuel was in the hospital, and there were no staircases he could fall down here, it would be fine. Also, as an active toddler who needed to be able to burn energy, this gave him a much better outlet than allowing him to crawl down the hallway of the hospital.

Satisfied to have thought the situation through, I set him in the walker and off we went. The nurses hooked him to a wireless monitor so that he could freely roam up and down the hallways. After the first few times taking him out, I noticed he really wanted to sprint when something excited him. To keep him from running out of our wing or into someone's room, I tied twenty feet of paracord to his walker.

Samuel has always had this 10,000-megawatt smile, just like his mother. We would make laps around the hallways of 7C, and Samuel would beam at the nurses and patients as he passed. They would return his smile and ask him how he was. He would laugh at this and sprint away, heading to the next nurse's station. Often, he would get so tickled at the nurses' attention to him, he would take off as fast as his baby legs would take him, jabbering and drooling and jutting forward with each step.

CHAPTER 9

ABLATIONS - THE FIRST EP

"JACOB WRESTLED THE ANGEL,
AND THE ANGEL WAS OVERCOME" ~ P.O.D.

As Samuel recovered from a fourth surgery, I heard a small whisper in my spirit one morning. I was declaring God's promises on my commute to work.

Over the summer, we did not have any major issues with Samuel's health. I also had no spiritual battles to fight – nothing to pray for, or to stand for in expectation. With Samuel's unexpected heart surgery in November, I was catapulted back into the fight. I quickly jumped into the mode of clinging to my confession and my belief that Samuel would live long in the land and grow strong in the land.

I took the time in my morning reading to tread back through the promises of scripture we stood on in Samuel's first 6 months of life. I was digging back into one of my favorites, 2 Chronicles 20, that tells of how God fought for Jehoshaphat. While driving to work that morning, I recited my positive confessions as I did every day on the way to work. I added a few, just for Samuel's situation. After I finished declaring "God fight's our battles for us," I heard a voice say in my soul, "I want you to fight."

I said nothing more. I drove on in silence, turning those words over in my mind.

It was early, and my mind was working slowly, but I felt confused. "How am I supposed to fight?" I thought. I chewed on the idea in the early morning light, with the hum of my wheels and Hillsong as the soundtrack to my musings.

When Samuel was first born, I had read a book by Mark Batterson called "The Circle Maker." It's a fantastic book on prayer. He opens the book by retelling a story from "The Book of Legends: Stories from the Talmud and Midrash." The story he shared was about a man named Honi, who prayed for rain. I highly recommend reading the rest of Mark Batterson's book, but I'm going to retell the story of Honi briefly:

There was a serious drought in Israel, and the people had heard of a man who could pray and successfully move God to bring rain. They called him to come pray for rain in Israel. When he came, he drew a circle in the dirt. He then knelt in the circle, and prayed loudly, "God, I am not moving from this circle until you bring rain." Soon, it began to drizzle. He prayed two more times, both times saying, "God, this is not the rain we need," first bringing a heavy rain and then finally bringing a proper rain to drench the land.

The people were overjoyed, but the priests were not. They wanted to excommunicate Honi for being so brazen in how he prayed to God. In the end, though, they couldn't deny that his prayer was both heard by God and was responsible for saving them. They relented.

Since before Samuel was born, I had been declaring God's promises over Samuel. By this point, I had withstood so much that my faith muscle – my ability to cling to a belief or an idea no matter the circumstances - was very strong. My mind chewed on this for a few days, and the Spirit slowly began to lead me through each step.

The first step was a passage from Izaiah 50:7, "and He set His face like flint." Flint is a hard rock. The edges tend to be sharp. It was used throughout history for knives and various other tools because of its ability to withstand impact. If it does happen to chip, it typically leaves a sharper surface.

That phrase was often linked to Jesus's decision to move forward towards Jerusalem, towards his torture and death ... and his resurrection. He knew what would oppose him and that his journey would be extremely difficult. He also knew what sat on the other side of his journey - his resurrection and the salvation of the world.

I knew Samuel would live long and grow healthy. My declaration, "Samuel will live long in the land and grow strong in the land," was where I was taking my stand, and I would not be moved. Like Jesus, I set my face like flint on what God had promised.

The second idea the Holy Spirit brought to my mind was a lyric from an old U2 song, one that P.O.D. had covered. The lyric was from "Bullet the Blue Sky", and went: "Jacob wrestled the angel, and the angel was overcome." This referenced the passage in Genesis 32 where Jacob wrestled the angel of God all night long, refusing to yield. In fact, the angel eventually gave up and hit Jacob's hip with a staff to get Jacob to leave him alone.

Even though I knew what God's word said about healing and Samuel's life, I couldn't help the feeling that maybe I was opposing the will of God. Let me be plain to you, I was not. God's word is explicit. But I still felt that way. This passage was incredibly encouraging. I'm not saying I'm better than Jacob, I'm just a man – but so was Jacob. If he would not give up, then neither would I. If I needed to wrestle God himself, then so be it.

There was a third premise that started to pop out in my morning Bible readings. It's summed up well here:

"No one whose hope is in you will ever be put to shame…"
Psalms 25:4 NIV

Through each step, I began to gain an understanding of what God wanted me to do. In short, as in Ephesians 6, He was calling me to "above all else, stand." In the coming months, I realized God was calling me to take on this bold role of faith like Jesus had done, to take my stand on my faith that Samuel would be well, and to viciously and adamantly stand on that faith.

To do that, I clung to the belief that Samuel would be well because it lined up with a promise of God in the Bible. That promise was mine because of Jesus's sacrifice. Because of this promise, I then suspended all belief in anything else. When I heard stories of other kids not making it, or the fears came that reminded me of those stories, I said, "No, let God's word be true and every man a liar (Romans 3:4)." When I worried if God wanted something else for our lives, I said, "No, God loves being reminded of His promises (Isaiah 62:6)." When I worried if I was believing wrong, that maybe God wasn't holding up His word, I said, "No, those who put their hope in God will not be put to shame (Psalms 25:3). I'm trusting in God to do good."

As we moved into December, we had some relief in one area.

Stephanie had been driving in to work three days a week to work in her office. When Samuel was home, this wasn't a problem. When Samuel was in the hospital, she wanted to be with him all she could. This meant she missed a decent amount of work. She often tried to make up hours at random times or on random days of the week. Gratefully, her work transferred her to a different department and allowed her to work remotely at this point in our journey. While we often wondered why they hadn't done so sooner, we were still extremely grateful that they allowed it.

Samuel's SVT was becoming difficult to manage with medicine alone, and this meant the hospital visits came frequently. In the month of December, Samuel went to Children's for SVT three separate times. This meant three separate stays in the hospital, attempting to get his medication adjusted.

With the trips to Children's becoming more frequent, and the dosing of Samuel's heart medicine become more difficult, Dr. Arora began to discuss attempting another ablation. This time he planned to use a catheter. By using a catheter, Dr. Arora and Dr. Beerman could go through an artery that ran from Samuel's thigh directly to his heart. After consulting with hospitals around the country and getting our approval, Dr. Arora put the timeframe tentatively in January or February.

On the 14th of December, less than three weeks after Samuel left the hospital from his fourth surgery, we had to rush Samuel to Children's for SVT – his first trip of the month. This trip, he was admitted directly to the Cardiac ICU, rather than getting a room in the cardiac wing first. His SVT broke that night, and he returned to a normal rhythm.

Apparently, he felt a little wild that night, as he was shaking the cage of his crib. While that might be a normal occurrence on most floors, there aren't too many wild toddlers in the Cardiac ICU. Most children are pre-operation, post-operation, or extremely sick. Every other time Samuel was in the Cardiac ICU, he had been one of those very sick children – either awaiting operation or recovering and after an operation. While we wanted to keep Samuel quiet so as not to disturb the other families, we couldn't help but laugh at the absurdity of him screaming wildly in the CICU. He was having a great time.

Since Samuel's SVT broke so quickly, we were able to bring him home after a few short days. However, he was back in SVT on the 20th. We went back to the Emergency Room where they once again insisted on trying to stop his SVT with Ice. The doctors were able to alter his medication enough again to get his heart to beat normally, and so he went home again two days later, on December 22nd.

Christmas Eve, we spent enjoying time with our kids. Izaiah had been with us from his last day of school before Christmas, and he was going back to his mom on Christmas day. We had opened presents early so we could all play with them as a family and so Izaiah had time with his presents.

We wrapped up the day with our normal nighttime routine: I gave Samuel his medicine and Izaiah his vitamins. Stephanie bathed Samuel, covering him in lotion, and I assisted in helping get them both dressed. Just before pulling them in bed with us to pray, Stephanie checked Samuel's heart rate with a stethoscope, as had become our custom. Stephanie counted his heart beats, holding her head still in tense anticipation.

"He's back in SVT," she sighed.

Exasperated, but knowing we needed to act, I asked Stephanie what she wanted to do.

We were exhausted. It was Christmas eve, and the third time this month. We just wanted a quiet, restful Christmas. Stephanie called and spoke with a doctor on-call at Children's.

After a short discussion, the doctor deemed it ok for us to wait until the morning to take him down. The doctor on-call suggested that we up Samuel's heart rhythm medication ourselves and bring him in after we got some rest.

The next day Stephanie took Samuel to Children's, and I met up with Izaiah's mother at our meet-up spot in Washington so he could spend the rest of his Christmas break with her. We spent the rest of the week after Christmas in the hospital.

I worked part of the week, trying to keep up with the medical decisions as best as I could over the phone. Stephanie was there with Samuel and was my go between on our medical questions to the nurses and doctors. Most mornings, as Dr. Arora was making his morning rounds, Stephanie would call me and let me listen in on the discussion and would make a point to have me ask any questions that I had.

Dr. Arora was facing a dilemma of his own at this point. He never told us directly of his struggle, but he would inform us of the calls and the research he was doing for the best ways to help Samuel. Dr. Arora was facing an unprecedented situation: he had never dealt with a child who had both a bad heart valve and SVT. Samuel was new territory for the seasoned doctor. He had faced hundreds of cases of

SVT and the hospital was incredibly familiar with valve replacements, yet they had not once faced the unique condition of both at the same time. The severity of each condition in Samuel made things even more pressing to make the right decisions. It would not be wise to continue to replace Samuel's heart valves every few months.

With every surgery to replace the valve, the surgeon had to cut away the scar tissue, healthy tissue that had turned hard, to make room for the new valve. Eventually, with the frequency of the surgeries, the surgeon would eventually cut away enough heart tissue to leave a hole in his heart. There was also the simple danger of heart surgery itself - one small mistake in any number of steps could kill Samuel, or at the least could leave him permanently injured.

The time to act was now. After pouring through papers, calling some of the best doctors around the country, and having many discussions amongst the Children's staff - Dr. Arora decided that he and Dr. Beerman wanted to attempt an ablation a few days into the New Year.

On the 28th, Stephanie noticed that Samuel was eating less and seemed much more lethargic. She had asked the resident and the nursing staff about it, but they seemed to brush off her concerns. We both had seen enough issues with his heart to know not to ignore major signs like this, so Stephanie continued to press. When I made it to the hospital after work, I discussed the situation with Stephanie and picked up where she had grown weary. We felt the best course of action was for them to perform an echo to make sure that his valve was functioning properly. The resident, a shorter dark-haired woman in her early 30's, did not think this was necessary.

We ended up getting into a lengthy discussion outside of Samuel's hospital room. I listened to her concerns, most of which were concerning gaining the approval needed from the doctors for an echo, as well as the medical necessity of it so late in the evening. I held my ground, continuing to gently but firmly press that we wanted an echo. Our incident in the PICU had shown us that we needed to stick to our guns. Eventually, she realized I was not changing my mind. She called the fellow on-call to come and administer an echo on Samuel.

It snowed that night - the first snow of the season. I walked the halls to burn energy as I waited for the doctor on-call to arrive. From the 7th floor, I could see the snow obscuring the sidewalks and streets below. As I watched the window, one car drove slowly down the street, leaving two black trails behind it and a bright white trail in front.

The on-call fellow took over an hour to arrive; the fresh snow had made the roads treacherous. He performed the echo himself. I stood watching, anxious to make sure my son was alright. My wife was exhausted and was sleeping in Samuel's room on the hospital futon.

As the fellow worked, I attempted to make small talk. I hated to have to ask him to drive to the hospital at 11 P.M. during the holidays to run this test. I felt bad about pushing so hard, and I felt bad for him having to leave his nice warm home. But I knew this was too important of a sign to ignore.

Surprisingly, Samuel's heart valve was functioning normally. I thanked him and apologized profusely, wishing him a happy holiday as he wrapped up. He still seemed frustrated to have been pushed to come in to run this test. Even though the test showed Samuel's valve was fine – a negative result also meant that we could rest easy that evening.

Over the next few days, Dr. Arora and Dr. Beerman settled on December 30th as the day to perform Samuel's ablation. On the 29th, Dr. Arora came to speak with us during his morning hospital rounds. He called the ablation an EP study, with EP being short for electro-physiological. The doctors would go through a catheter in his leg, making their way through his body to the veins in Samuel's heart. They would also be using an echo to view the heart and the catheter's position. When the catheter was in the proper place, they would heat the tip and cauterize one small spot on his heart nerves. They were hoping to hit the nerve that was causing the SVT.

Dr. Arora explained it to us quickly while still managing to cover all the necessary information. He always spoke quickly and with a smile, yet he was also extremely patient with our questions. He had been talking to the doctors at Boston Children's where he had done his residency or fellowship (or both). He had been busy pouring through case studies and had been making calls to many other doctors around the country, trying to find the best treatment plan for Samuel. The humility of this man astounded me. He was arguably one of the best in his field, yet he was still seeking the wisdom and experiences of other doctors. He and Dr. Beerman would be performing the procedure. Samuel was slated first the next morning.

When the next day came, Samuel ended up getting bumped to 11 A.M., as there was an emergency heart surgery that needed to go first.

When it was finally Samuel's turn, we prepped for Samuel's procedure as we always did by walking him to the anesthesiologist and praying over him and for the entire surgical team. When we were ready to let him go, they whisked him off to start his procedure. Dr. Arora had informed us it would take somewhere between 4 and 6 hours. Stephanie's parents were with us, as they were for every procedure. We kept my parents in the loop as much as possible. My parents lived five hours away and had a farm and farm animals to tend. This made it difficult for them to be there for every procedure, but they were with us as much as they possible could be. Often, they were staying at our house during hospital visits or procedures, taking care of Izaiah if he was with us and our dog Gracie.

After getting settled, I realized it was close to lunchtime. Turning to Steph, I asked, "Hey babe, want to go with me to get lunch?"

She shook her head no from where she had taken her position. She was lying across some of the seats in the waiting area, anxiety written on her face. I could see the tension in her body.

I responded, asking, "Are you sure?" I had hoped to get her mind on anything else.

"I'm sorry babe," she replied after a moment. "My nerves are too shot to eat."

Turning to Steph's parents, I extended the offer to them, "Would you guys like to go?"

Both decided to join, and we went to the cafeteria to grab lunch.

After returning, we spent the rest of the day staring. Staring at books, staring at phones, staring at TVs, and staring at each other. We were in good spirits, and we were less stressed about this procedure than we had been about the others. It's difficult to do much of anything significant at times like those. On top of it all, the months of procedures were taking a toll on all of us, especially Steph and myself. We had both gained a lot of weight, and our stress levels were constantly off the charts.

At three in the afternoon, four hours after Samuel had been pulled back, we began to wonder how the procedure was going. The screen that showed his status was too vague to make out how soon he would be done. Almost as if hearing our questions, a nurse came by to give us an update from the operating room that everything was going well. They were still continuing to map the pathways (their word for each of the nerves on Samuel's heart). At 5 in the afternoon, the waiting room started to thin out. We grabbed dinner in shifts, making sure to have someone in the waiting room in case a doctor needed us. The hours stretched on. We were receiving updates every two hours or so. As we approached 7 P.M, we were beginning to worry. Samuel had been under for eight hours, yet there was nothing we could do but wait. At approximately 9:45 P.M, Dr. Arora and Dr. Beerman came out. Both looked drained, but confident.

"We think we did it!" Dr. Arora said with a large, weary smile. He continued, "Samuel is very tired and will need a few days to recover."

"Why is that?" Stephanie questioned. We both had assumed that the recovery for this would be very short, as they weren't cutting Samuel open.

"Well, Samuel still had to be on a heart bypass machine. He's very tired. This was a really long day and a long procedure. But we think we got it."

We nodded, understanding. "But you think you did?" I replied.

"We think we did," he responded.

That was enough for us.

In a cruel twist, the triumph was incredibly short lived. Within 24 hours, Samuel's SVT had returned. To top it off, his recovery from this procedure took longer this time than any of the others. Apparently, the length of time he spent on anesthetics as well as on the heart bypass machine took a big toll on his tiny body. To make matters worse, the listlessness and lack of appetite he was exhibiting before surgery was the start of RSV, which we found out as Samuel was recovering in the CICU. Similar to the common cold, RSV is a respiratory infection. While this typically isn't a serious condition for adults, this can be fatal for an infant. Recovering from surgery made it more so. Samuel took almost two full days before he was awake.

Even after he woke, he seemed uncommonly fatigued. Due to the rough recovery, the medical team did not take him off the bipap machine within the first day of surgery, as they typically had done after most procedures.

Thankfully, between the massive amount of people praying and the incredible hospital staff in the CICU, Samuel was in the best possible place he could be. Our church, and churches all over the country, had someone asking their congregation to pray for Samuel.

Finally, on January 4th, five days after his EP study, Samuel came off the bipap. The doctors were still struggling to get Samuel's SVT under control. They chose the 6th, the first Wednesday of the year, for Samuel to go in for another ablation, but this time they would perform it surgically.

To keep from adding to the scar tissue on his chest, Dr. Arora and Dr. Morell wanted to go in through his side, between the bones of his rib cage. They also wouldn't need as large of a cut to gain access. It was a little rough having Samuel go in for another surgery when he hadn't fully recovered from the last procedure. However, we agreed to it, as we did not want him to clot up another valve, which would cause another valve replacement.

We went through the same routine for Samuel's surgery this time as any other. This time they took Samuel back in the afternoon. After a few hours, Stephanie and I went for dinner at the cafeteria. When we returned, Dr. Arora found us and pulled us into one of the small conference rooms.

The room resembled a tiny office, but not much larger than a broom closet. There were four of these conference rooms that sat on the edge of the surgical waiting room. They were very tiny, with yellow wallpaper, and a small "L" shaped desk. There was just enough room between the end of the desk that jutted out to walk past. There were heavy wooden doors at each end, and three black chairs in the room – two on the side towards the waiting room, and one on the inside of the "L".

Stephanie, her mom, and I followed Dr. Arora into this small room. While he always seemed to talk quickly, he seemed to be just a little more rushed than normal. While we were determining how to arrange ourselves, I gave Stephanie and her mom the two chairs closest to the waiting room. I offered to stand so Dr. Arora could have the chair on the inside of the "L", but he insisted we all sit. He pushed the chair around for me and he proceeded to kneel at the desk, positioning himself across from us to discuss his plans so he could stay at eye level. The humility of the gesture was not lost on me.

"We want to try a riskier catheter procedure," he began. "There was a certain area we wanted to ablate before in the last procedure, but it was too dangerous to attempt with a catheter. Given the circumstances of how we would be ablating it, there was a small risk of rupturing one of the arteries on the heart. Normally, this would be hard to detect, and could be potentially fatal."

We were slightly stunned at all of this, not sure where he was going.

"The reason it can be fatal," he continued, "is because if we caused a break in the vessels - the pericardium, or the sack around the heart, would fill with blood and start to constrict the heart. This in turn would cause heart failure."

"We want to attempt this now with the pericardium opened," he continued on, "as we think we have the best chance of success at ablating the right nerve."

I looked at Stephanie in shock. I wanted time to think about it, to pray about it. She, however, jumped right in, "Do it!"

I was a little taken aback at her abruptness, and the lack of conferring with me. I tapped her on the arm and whispered that I wanted to talk before agreeing. She wanted none of it. Despite my quiet protests, she said again, "Do it."

Dr. Arora looked at me, and I reluctantly nodded. This was all too much for me to process.

When Dr. Arora left the room, I felt angry at Stephanie for not discussing this with me. I tried to talk with her, but she brushed it off. She insisted it was the best thing for him and she didn't want to wait for me to decide. Frustrated, I finally decided to let it go. It wasn't worth the fight considering the severity of what we were facing.

Letting go of the anger took a while. It was an hour and a half before Dr. Arora and Dr. Beerman emerged from the operating room, but to me it only felt like a few moments. This time, they didn't bother with bringing us into a conference room. The waiting room was empty, and it was very dark outside. They both came to us where we had been sitting for almost 10 hours.

"We are sure we got it," Dr. Arora exclaimed. The elation in their posture countered the weariness caused by the length of the day; they were confident that the procedure was a success. While Stephanie and I should have been elated, the length of time we had been fighting left our emotions were muted. Both the successes and the failures were ignored, as we plodded forward in stubborn resolve to survive.

CHAPTER 10

PARKING

"I LIKE A MAN WHO GRINS WHEN HE FIGHTS."
~ WINSTON CHURCHILL

As Samuel's recovery stretched through the first few weeks of January, we pressed on in our struggle to balance the rest of our life with Samuel's massive amount of medical attention. We were grateful that Samuel recovered much quicker from the surgical ablation than he had from the catheter ablation the previous week.

Unfortunately, we had already been in the hospital for over a week by the time Samuel had his surgical ablation. This time, Samuel had spent his entire stay in the CICU, which meant only one of us could stay in his hospital room. Sleeping arrangements consisted of an old fold out chair pushed into a back corner beside one stack of monitors and medical drip machines. The room was a typical ICU room in that it had glass walls and curtains to give someone a bit of privacy. The bathroom was a shared bathroom with one shower that sat out in the CICU waiting room. The door stood to the left of the CICU check-in desk.

Stephanie slept the entire week in the CICU, and I continued to make my driving circuit between the hospital, work, and our house.

Izaiah went back to his mom on Christmas day, and my parents had left for southern West Virginia. By this point in our journey, our dog was staying with Stephanie's parents all the time. Any time I spent at home was mainly to sleep, and occasionally to wash clothes. The only other option for me was to sleep in the CICU lobby. I chose to sleep at home.

Most years I would have been off work and enjoying time resting between Christmas and New Year's. I typically spent the time planning out the next year's goals, looking back over the prior year's failures and accomplishments, and spending copious amounts of time with my wife and children. Instead, I chose not to waste an hour of off time from work, continuing my normal work and life patterns.

At this point in my life, everything was a fight. I fought for Samuel's health and to keep my head above water; I fought to keep my job. I fought to find time with my wife, and I wanted to fight every single person who disagreed with me.

I struggled to make sure I kept my fighting focused on the most important things and didn't lash out at the things that were inconsequential. I am a big farm boy. I knew if I were to get angry, I could physically hurt someone.

After hitting six feet at age 14, I realized I was a lot stronger than most people my age. I spent most of my life avoiding situations that could make me really angry so that I wouldn't hurt someone who I didn't want to hurt or scare someone who I didn't want to scare. The downside of that was I often ended up avoiding conflict where I should have stood up for myself, but I didn't feel I could trust myself if I lost my temper. It's not enough for me to know that I am powerful enough to physically fight if a situation warranted; I need to know that

I am powerful enough to keep myself calm and under control in an escalating situation where avoiding a fight is prudent.

As Samuel recovered from surgery number five, I got the opportunity to see just how far I had come in my ability to keep under control.

Parking at Children's Hospital could use some work. The hospital is located on the outer limits of the city of Pittsburgh, so every bit of real estate is expensive. Parking is limited to the side of the street and one of Children's three garages. The first garage is their emergency room garage. This sits under the main lobby. The second garage is called mid-campus. As the name suggests, it sits in the middle of the hospital block and separates the main part of the hospital and from the Ronald McDonald house and some of the conference rooms. The third garage is an employee garage and is also where long term patients can stay. Long term patients meant a patient who had been in the hospital for 21 days.... consecutively. There were many times that Samuel was in the hospital just shy of 3 weeks. However, we only reached the free parking threshold once. One time we managed to be in the hospital for 18 days, were discharged, and then back within the same week for another 7 days. We were still not granted free parking. It had to be consecutive.

The parking for parents was a discounted rate from what most other visitors paid. A normal visitor maxes out somewhere between $7 and $10 a day, while the discounted daily parking rate was $5. It wasn't terrible, but it still added up quickly. Samuel was in the hospital between 100 and 180 days. We struggled to find creative ways to keep from having to pay for parking. I would often park on the street after work if I could find a spot, as on-street parking was free after 6 p.m. Sometimes, it was easier just to pay to park in the garage.

In one of the earlier visits to take Samuel down for SVT, Stephanie took Samuel by herself to the emergency room. I stayed back with Izaiah, as it was bedtime, and we didn't want to take both boys if we could keep from it.

Stephanie had parked in the temporary parking spaces near the entrance to the emergency room for Children's Hospital. She took Samuel inside and checked him in, where the nurses quickly ushered them back to a room.

The emergency rooms at Children's have adult size beds. You must specifically ask for a crib to be brought to your room, and they aren't always available. This meant that we were constantly hovering over Samuel to make sure he didn't roll off the bed. We wouldn't have left him alone in the ER, but if only one of us were with him there, we might have needed to do so.

I've already mentioned the standard methods of getting Samuel out of SVT, which are almost as bad as the thoughts of having another surgery. They always insisted on using ice to attempt to get Samuel out of SVT before using the medicine to stop and restart his heart.

One would think that the parking attendants would recognize that they worked at a hospital, and the parents there were under a lot of stress. Maybe they might give the parents a little grace. This was sadly not the case. On this visit, a parking attendant barged into my son's room to demand Stephanie immediately move her car from the temporary parking to normal parking.

They did not care that she had an infant child in the emergency room with heart issues, nor did they care that he was lying on a bed that couldn't contain him and which meant he fall on to the hard floor. The nurses were not able to stop and watch him. My wife told me about the incident later, but I never fully had the chance to address it with the hospital staff. We had bigger issues to fight.

As Samuel recovered from his ablations, I got the chance to address the issue.

Samuel's surgical ablation was on Wednesday, January 6th. His recovery was progressing well. On Friday, however, Stephanie came down with a stomach bug. I sent her home to recover, and I stayed at the hospital with Samuel in her place. Fortunately, she got sick on a weekend that we didn't have Izaiah, so I was able to stay at the hospital all weekend without interruption.

I spent the days watching over Samuel's care, playing with him when he felt good enough and reading or talking with friends when he was tired. By Monday, Samuel was moved up to the stepdown unit in 7A. Stephanie was still sick, so I coordinated with some volunteers and with Stephanie's family to make sure someone was with Samuel during the day. I drove to work from the hospital in the morning after a volunteer arrived.

I was fortunate enough that Samuel was back in the stepdown unit on 7A. The rooms in 7A had a private bathroom, and I was able to shower in the room before leaving for work. I ate whatever I could find donated in the communal kitchen. After work, I drove straight to the hospital. I relieved whoever had stayed with him for the day. Between the sleeping arrangements, my concern for my wife and Samuel, and the level of stress at my job, I was beyond physically and mentally exhausted.

By Tuesday evening, Stephanie was badly missing her baby boy. She called the doctor on call working with Samuel. After some discussion, they concluded that she wasn't contagious, and she would be fine to see him.

When Stephanie arrived at the hospital, she was still feeling weak and sick to her stomach. I told her I would meet her out in front of the hospital and drive her car to the garage. That enabled her to walk in through the lobby instead of having to take the long walk through the hospital from the parking garage.

Stephanie was thrilled to see Samuel, and he was ecstatic to see his Mommy. The visit was short but joyful, as they both were recovering from their respective medical problems.

The front entrance to Children's is set back from the road about 50 feet. There are three lanes that go under the front of the building, which is two stories high. The cover allows one to pick up and drop off at the front entrance without having to fight traffic and weather. The area is well lit, and the lobby's floor-to-ceiling windows and white interior make it a welcoming entrance into the hospital. There is also a valet booth that is manned all day that assists with parking. It is not a courtesy service, though, and one must pay extra for valet.

When Stephanie grew too tired to stay longer, I offered to help her as much as possible. "You stay here," I said. "I will go get the car, park it under the overpass, and come up to help you down."

"Are you sure you won't have any problems leaving the car there?" Stephanie questioned, knowing how particular the attendants were about parking.

"It will be fine," I reassured her, "You are getting over being sick. They shouldn't have any problem with it." I hoped that I was right.

Between the circumstances and my persuasion ability, I would be able to get security to agree with allowing me to leave Steph's car sitting under the overpass for ten minutes. My wife was sick, we had been here off and on for over a year, and it was after 8 p.m.: why would they deny us? I thought it over in my head as I walked to the elevator, still feeling uneasy. I stuffed the feeling down.

I rode down to the first floor and stopped at the security desk. The security guards rotated every hour, so it never seemed you saw the same one each pass. At this point, I had come to know them all. The one behind the small podium that evening was a tall blonde woman. She had always seemed friendly but quiet.

"Hello," I said gently, "I wanted to ask you for something." I was hoping to win as much favor with the security guard as possible, so I made sure my tone and speech were gentle. "My wife is recovering from a stomach bug, and she is here visiting my son. I don't want her to have to walk through the hospital to get the car. Could I park it under the underpass so I can walk her down?"

"Sure," she said, nodding and straightening herself up in her chair. "That shouldn't be a problem."

"Thank you," I replied. The ease with which she granted my request was welcomed. I was exhausted, and I didn't feel like fighting. I was as grateful for the ease of approval as I was for the approval itself.

I made my way to the back of the hospital and into the parking garage. I started Steph's car, pulled it out onto the street and under the hospital overpass. I eased just before the doors so I wouldn't be in the way. At 8 P.M., there was only one other car in the underpass.

I could see the full lobby to my right as I put the car in park. The lobby crowd had thinned from the 20 to 30 people who were constantly in and out during the day, to less than 10. One family sat in the seating area to the left of the six doored entrance. Two or three other people dealt with guest passes or parking. The security guard sat at a podium near the elevators and two attendants sat at the check-in desk.

I turned the car off and stepped out, locking the car doors behind me.

As I stepped towards the door, one of the younger valets yelled to get my attention. "Are you going to park that there?"

I was not in the mood to deal with a parking attendant. I responded shortly, "Yes, talk to security," and briskly walked towards the door. I hoped they would radio security and get the all-clear.

As I walked through the bright, open lobby towards the security desk, I caught a glimpse of the one valet relaying to the lead valet what had transpired. He listened for a moment, and then took off after me. He was a short man with a larger belly, probably late forties to mid-fifties. His short legs worked back and forth comically as he rushed towards the door in a full-on speed walk.

He burst through the lobby doors, yelling at me as soon as he had the second door open. "Hey!" he bellowed across the lobby.

I continued walking towards the guard desk, ignoring him. I hoped security would step in to handle it.

"Hey, I need to talk with you!" he shouted, crossing the lobby quickly. The woman at the security desk was silent.

I was trying to avoid this. I knew being this tired, I might not be able to control my mouth or my actions. I stopped just beside the guard's desk, realizing I was not going to be able to avoid having this conversation. I set both bags Stephanie had brought me on the ground. I pulled my shoulders back and turned to face this man. He stopped a few steps away.

"Hey, I need to talk with you. You can't park your car there!" he shouted angrily at me; his face contorted at this egregious act.

I nodded toward security and said, "I spoke with security, and they said it was fine."

He then turned on the security guard, the same woman I had spoken to a few minutes prior. He began shouting at her, something about how they were supposed to speak with him first. She recoiled slightly from his anger and mumbled something in reply.

At this point, I snapped.

I stood even straighter and took one large step to close the distance between him and myself. As I stood towering over him, uncomfortably close, he stopped talking.

"We do need to talk," I said, locking eyes with him.

He froze, realizing he had pressed too far, and took a small step back.

"What!?" he startled; his once booming voice was now restrained.

"We **do** need to talk," I repeated, pausing for effect. "A few months ago, my wife came down to the E.R. with my son, and you harassed her while she was in the E.R. about where she parked."

He began backpedaling; his voice now a mumble, "It wasn't me." He stuttered, "It … it was one of my guys."

I stepped towards him as he was backing away, "Well, you are in charge of them, and we need to talk."

At this point, he tucked tail and disappeared from the lobby.

Seeing that I wouldn't have any more trouble from him, I turned to the security guard. I nodded, and I waited for her to nod back. She eventually regained her composure and gave me a nod.

Satisfied, I grabbed my bags and continued to the elevator. I was relieved to know that I wasn't in trouble, and I wouldn't be fighting anyone else that night.

I called Stephanie while she was on her way home and recounted the story. Surprised at my actions, she insisted that I had had enough of staying at the hospital at that point. The next morning, she relieved me from staying with Samuel and stayed with him for the rest of his stay.

While many may ask if the confrontation was necessary, I felt I finally could trust myself. There were three areas I didn't always trust myself to handle well in confrontation. The first was knowing that, when pressed, I did not back down. The second, instead of taking the attack personally, I simply took it for what it was – an attack. It didn't affect my image of who I was. The third was knowing that I could trust myself to be restrained and not let my anger take me too far. I know it sounds strange, but I was incredibly proud of how I handled the situation. I felt I could trust myself as a warrior – a fighter who adhered to his ethical code.

CHAPTER 11

PIGS AND ABLATIONS - ANOTHER EP

"For Great is Your love, reaching to the heavens, Your Faithfulness reaches to the skies." ~ Psalm 57:10 NIV

Samuel was released from the hospital on January 13th. While back at work the next day, I sat at lunch and journaled. The company I worked for was in a business park in Robinson, a township of Pittsburgh. It was the first of a few office buildings after a mile of box stores and small rows of storefronts. I often went to one of the restaurants, coffee shops, or a cigar lounge to sit and clear my head and get out of the office.

I typically like to process my thoughts verbally, but during Samuel's journey, I kept myself closed off from many people. While I didn't mind other people knowing my struggles with Samuel, I wanted people who spoke into my life to be someone with as strong or a stronger faith in God's promises than I had. I needed boldness, not sympathy, and definitely not fear. This meant that at many times, I wasn't telling all my friends and coworkers, and sometimes not my parents, all the intimate details of our struggle or my personal battles. Stephanie kept people updated through social media on the major events. Even that was more than I wanted at times, but it proved mostly positive.

Even with a smaller social circle, we had many people by our side. Both Stephanie's parents and mine were always faithful to help, and Stephanie's sister came any time we needed. Many people on our Amway team were also supportive, as well as a few other friends who I had met since moving to Pittsburgh. A few people Stephanie knew from church were constantly helping her. Quite a few even went out of their way to give us money, to bring food, or to come visit us.

One couple, Dane and Karen, visited us almost every single time we were in the hospital. Because of this, they hold a special place in our hearts. They would often bring us food and simply sit with us. They never attempted to quote scripture, to offer something "wise," or to offer advice. It must have been very uncomfortable for them at times; we were often too overwhelmed to even speak. When we didn't talk, they didn't try to force small talk; they just gave us a smile and sat awkwardly with us.-

Most of the time, when I needed to process my grief and refocus my thoughts, I kept it private. I knew I needed to be heard to process this grief, but I was cautious. Too many people who want to listen also have no problem sharing their own doubts and fears. I knew that Jake had a lot on his plate, and I wasn't sure he would be ok hearing my emotions. I knew many other friends I had either didn't know how to process this emotion or didn't know how to help me frame my thoughts properly. So, I turned to my journal.

On this Thursday afternoon, as I was mentally preparing for the weekend, I sat at a coffee chain, expressing myself to the page in writing. I focused my words and my thoughts on God's words and His promises. I chose to focus on my future. At this moment, I believed fully that this last ablation was a complete success, and our journey with Samuel's health challenges was over. I had been clinging to my dreams and desires. I knew God had put them there for a purpose – for His purpose.

After one of the most intense battles over Samuel's health, one that included oppression from work, overzealous parking attendants, assaults on my wife's physical health, and setback after setback in my son's health progression; I desperately needed to be around people of faith. My business team was hosting a conference that weekend, 9 hours away, in Nashville, Tennessee. I did not want to leave my wife and my son alone at the house for the weekend. One of my business partners and close friends was getting married that weekend as well, and I did not want to miss his wedding. However, I knew, more than anything else, I needed to be with the men and women of faith who had given me the strongest guidance through Samuel's ordeals. Many of those people would be speaking at that weekend conference.

While I didn't admit it to my journal, I was raw. I was emotionally, mentally, and physically drained. On Friday, after swinging through Morgantown to see Izaiah, I made the long and dreary trip through Ohio, Kentucky, and into Tennessee. I travelled by myself, which allowed me to stop frequently. The frequent breaks pushed my arrival time back, and it began to look like I was going to be late. I failed to realize that I passed into a new time zone, which allowed me to get there a few minutes before the start at 7 P.M.

One of the things most people don't realize about conferences like this: there aren't a lot of new things to learn. It is more what is lined out in Romans 12:2, which talks about the constant renewing of your mind. When you are living in faith, and you are hoping for something that you currently don't see in the physical, your mind needs to be constantly renewed. While these leaders who I had associated with over the years were teaching me business principles, but in reality, they were training me to have faith in God's word and in hope for my future. I had searched far and wide to find other people who taught faith this way and had an opportunity for me, but I was never able to find it. What my LTD team offered was unique.

One event from the weekend sticks out in my mind. While standing in line for the restroom during a break on Friday evening, I struck up a conversation with one of the speakers. His name was Josh Roby. Aside from being a literal rocket scientist, he had also achieved a significant level of success in his Amway business.

I was exhausted from the trip as well as the intense mental journey I had struggled through over the last few months, but I was excited to get the chance to say hello. I spoke up as we stood in line. "Josh, you gave a fantastic talk," I said, pushing a smile through my weariness. Josh had been one of the speakers that evening.

"Thank you," he replied with a huge smile. "How was your trip in?"

Briefly thinking over what I wanted to discuss, I subtly let him know the struggle it was to leave, "It was a decent trip in, but it was hard to leave my wife and son."

"That's why you are here – you are working to free up more time in the future," he replied. I knew he was wanting to be positive and had no idea the struggle we with which we were dealing. He was wanting to keep me focused on why I was here, so I could move forward.

I nodded, realizing I would probably need to be a bit more transparent. "No, it's not that." I hesitated, not wanting to overshare.

I proceeded slowly so as not to dump out all the weight of my circumstances on Josh, "My youngest just had heart surgery."

Josh's face changed from smiling to serious. He asked a few questions, and then he offered to pray for me. There in the grey hallway beside a hotel ballroom, Josh put his hand on my shoulder and started praying. We were the only ones left in the hallway at this point, as everyone else had returned to the conference room. After he prayed, he continued talking to me for a few minutes, encouraging me to persevere. I was honored by the amount of time he spent with me.

The trip home from that weekend was dreary. The flat plains and rolling hills of Tennessee, Kentucky, and Ohio were brown and yellow from the dead grass. The grey skies and roads, the leafless trees dotting the landscape, all echoed the state of my soul. I wept often during the 9-hour trip, processing months of hurt. My soul felt tight, bound between not wanting to confess my fears and needing to process my emotions.

That Sunday I also watched a movie called "Little Boy." It's about World War 2 and a child whose one and only friend, his dad, goes off to war. It's an incredible example of a kid who has childlike faith. I wept after watching it, realizing I was the child and Samuel, my son was the dad. He would be back to normal again. The journey of faith is often like that – barren and filled with setbacks, and brief but intense moments of incredible miracles.

Having had a weekend away to draw from positive and godly people, and some time to myself to process my emotions, I returned to my home with a new sense of strength. Over the next few days, I began to plot out moving forward in my business and our life with an expectation that we were finished with Samuel's medical procedures for a long time.

Through the rest of January and into February, I slowly returned to my daily routines. Grief takes time to process. Sometimes I was able to move forward while hurting. Other times, the hurt was too big, and I needed to process that grief.

By the first week of February, I had processed enough of my grief to move forward. I also was implementing a new practice. Every time I was hurt, I was going to take those hurts to God, aggressively. In my mind, I knew we were through with Samuel's medical journey, and I could finally move forward.

The day after my birthday in the second week of February, we noticed Samuel wasn't acting normal. Once again, his eating was off, and he was lethargic. We had not been regularly checking Samuel's heart rate because we assumed that the ablations were successful. We began looking for a stethoscope to check his heart rate. Typically, there were two within arm's reach in our bedroom and one readily available in Samuel's room. In our laxness, we had not touched them in over a month. The cheap yellow tubes were typically easy to spot, hanging from the rack behind our door or sitting on top of Steph's dresser. Somehow, all had disappeared.

While Stephanie dug around in our room for a stethoscope, I picked Samuel up and held his chest up to my ear. I started counting the beats as I looked at my watch and listened, but I didn't have to count them. Hearing the first three beats, I could tell by how close they were together that his heart was beating at double speed. I looked at Stephanie, and said, "I think he's in SVT."

Her face showed frustration and a hint of anger, "Are you sure?" All our hopes for a return to normalcy hinged on the success of the ablation, at stopping his SVT.

"I'm pretty sure," I replied, knowing Steph's frustration.

She stepped in to make sure Samuel didn't fall off the bed, checking him out as she did. I went to search for a stethoscope in his room. Samuel was 15 months old. Although he could crawl well, all his surgeries had delayed his development and he wasn't close to walking.

After a few minutes, I returned with a stethoscope. "Here you go," I blurted.

She responded tersely, "I already have one." She must have found one somewhere in the room, and I noticed it sitting beside the bed. She stood over him, staring at the wall. The frustration in her posture had been a constant since Samuel's fourth surgery in November. It had started to fade after Samuel's ablation a month ago. Now it was back as though it had never left.

My own frustration reared its ugly head, and I became annoyed with the terseness of her response. "Did you check him?" I said tersely in return. After I spoke, I noticed the cheap yellow stethoscope sitting next to Samuel on our bed.

"Yes," she said continuing to stand, tense and unmoving.

Our conversation turned to the task at hand.

"Do you want me to go with you to take him down?" I asked, talking about the hospital.

She replied, "You don't have to."

"I don't mind," I said nodding.

"You have to work in the morning," she said through the fatigue.

Seeing the exhaustion on her face, and the tenseness, I knew my wife needed me. "I'll go," I said, giving my best smile.

We packed a quick bag for the two of us and made our way down in the dark cold night to Children's, again.

I stayed at the hospital with Stephanie that night, driving in to work a little late the next morning. I took a short lunch since I started work late. While on my shortened lunch, I took a few moments on Facebook to share with my friends what was on my heart. My morning reading had been on Psalm 57.

David is writing this song in a cave. He is hiding from the king of Israel, King Saul, who has gone crazy. David was not only his greatest warrior; he was the best friend of his son, the husband of his daughter, and the man who had taken care of him when he was tormented. David was extremely loyal and was King Saul's best asset.

While in this cave, David is taking a familiar refrain. Over the past month, I had begun to notice that David took on a similar pattern in many of the Psalms that he wrote.

He begins by crying out, exasperated. He continues laying out his feelings, fears, and frustrations through the next six verses.

> *"1 Have mercy on me, my God, have mercy on me,*
> *for in you I take refuge.*
> *I will take refuge in the shadow of your wings*
> *until the disaster has passed." ~Psalm 57:1 NIV*

He then pivots in his focus. He begins declaring his trust in his heavenly Father and continues on to ask for His protection.

"I will take refuge in the shadow of your wings
until the disaster has passed."

But as he is declaring God's protection and God's vengeance on those who would harm his servant, David progresses to losing himself in praise to His God:

"7 My heart, O God, is steadfast,
my heart is steadfast.
I will sing and make music.
8 Awake, my soul!
Awake, harp and lyre!
I will awaken the dawn.
9 I will praise you, Lord, among the nations;
I will sing of you among the peoples.
10 For great is your love, reaching to the heavens;
your faithfulness reaches to the skies.
11 Be exalted, O God, above the heavens;
let your glory be over all the earth." ~ Psalm 57:7-11 NIV

It was in this that I found strength. After quoting this passage of scripture in my journal, I continued sharing my heart:

"I honestly thought this last ablation was it. I thought we were done, and we could focus on other battles, but we are drawn back in to fighting for our son's health.
"However, we will get back up to fight, and we will win. Prov 24:16 (NIV) says 'For a righteous man falls seven times, and rises again, But the wicked stumble in time of calamity.'

"Our God is good and faithful, and Samuel will live a long and healthy and normal life. God has delivered Samuel from much scarier and (He has) stood true to His promise to be a fortress our children can stand in."

I was hurting, but I was learning to deal with my hurts and get back up so I could keep moving forward. I was finding that, in order to keep moving forward, I needed to ignore the small hurts but deal with the bigger hurts. To deal, I needed to grieve. To grieve, I did as David did.

In my frustration and pain, I told God how much that I was hurting. I let it all out, sharing with him how I felt. I then pivoted to declaring God's promises and God's character over my situation. I then finished by praising God.

We were in the hospital for over a week, through Valentine's Day, attempting to get Samuel's heart regulation medications back on track. After the surgery, Dr. Arora had taken Samuel completely off his heart regulation medication.

Stephanie and I celebrated the holiday at the hospital cafeteria, eating sushi and pizza. We made the best of the circumstances, but the disappointment of Samuel's continued SVT colored our impromptu date night.

The day after Valentine's Day, Samuel was released from the hospital with new medication schedules. We fell back into the routine of wondering if this medication would hold for months, or if we would be back at Children's Hospital within the week.

I was finally coming to a point where I no longer operated on the fear that something bad was going to happen, which had been killing my productivity.

On March 9th, I took a moment after work to gather my thoughts and rest. It was Wednesday, 66 degrees and sunny. After a cold Pittsburgh winter, this felt like shorts weather. I sat out on our patio and smoked a cigar, letting the warm air and the hint of the coming spring ease my mind. I sat with a book and my journal open. As I read, the fragrant cigar smoke mixed with the smell of damp dirt and sun. The evening was still, and the last rays of the day painted the bricks of the houses a bright orange. The grass had already begun to turn a little greener. As I sat, taking it all in, a strong breeze kicked up. I felt my spirit stir with the breeze, and I heard the Holy Spirit say, "There is a wind of change coming."

His voice was welcome, but I also didn't want to misinterpret where God was moving. "Where, God?" I asked out loud. I was smiling and glad to hear from Him.

"In you," was the response. As I thought on this, I felt in my spirit a reminder of Ephesians 3:20:

"Now to him who is able to do immeasurably more than all we ask or imagine, according to his power that is at work within us." ~ Ephesians 3:20 NIV

I didn't know what to make of this, but I wrote it down in my journal. If only I had known what God was about to so rapidly put into motion.

Over the next few days, Samuel started to grow lethargic and fussy, almost as if he had started to develop a cold or the flu. By Saturday, he started vomiting and having diarrhea. Samuel was scheduled for another EP study the following Wednesday. The EP study was another name for an ablation – the procedure to fix his racing heart.

Samuel continued to vomit and have diarrhea throughout the day. Towards the afternoon, Stephanie grew concerned he would get dehydrated. After a short discussion with me, she decided to take Samuel down to Children's for fluids. We had been so focused on his vomiting and dehydration, that we didn't think to check Samuel's heart rate.

At the hospital, they checked his pulse, weight, and height. He had gained weight and grew taller in the month since he was there. He was also in SVT again, his heart racing over 150 beats per minute. He was moved from the ER and admitted to the heart wing in 7C. Maybe the doctors noticed more going on than we could grasp, but he was moved that same day to the CICU.

While he was there, the staff ran another echo on him and found out his mechanical valve was no longer working. A blood clot had once again clotted the valve, keeping it from opening and closing properly. The doctors started to plan out an operation for the next few days. As the day progressed, so did the deterioration of Samuel's conditions and the doctors' plans. By evening, Dr. Arora was calling in the surgeon, Dr. Morell.

That same afternoon, Dr. Arora had asked for our thoughts on giving Samuel a pig valve. Stephanie was comfortable with it; she had spoken to adults in the hospital who had pig valves, and they were very pleased with the results. We had no pressing concerns, so he walked us through the pros and cons.

First, Samuel was finally large enough for a tissue valve (in this case, pig tissue). Second, with a tissue valve, Samuel wouldn't need blood thinners. The tradeoff was that the valve might not last as long. Tissue valves typically have a 5-year life, compared to 10-20 years for the mechanical valves. Despite not needing the blood thinners, Dr. Arora chose the more cautious route and kept Samuel on them anyway. Samuel had clotted out so many heart valves, Dr. Arora didn't want to take the risk.

That evening, after Dr. Morell arrived, they took Samuel back for his sixth heart surgery. We waited as we had each of the prior five times, but this time it seemed as rapid as the rest of this hospital visit. It seemed to be less than an hour before the nurse called us back to see Samuel. Dr. Arora met us on our way, as he sometimes had done. This time, he met us with a surprise.

"We successfully ablated," he said with simple confidence, as if he was telling us two and two were four.

"Ablated?" Stephanie and I asked. We were surprised by the news. Samuel was in surgery for less than two hours, and they had done a valve replacement and an ablation? We were incredulous. We hadn't realized they were planning to perform an ablation again, or if we did know, we had missed it through the numbness.

"Yes," he continued, "the last ablation, there was an area we couldn't get to when we had him open. This time, we had a chance to go right in and take care of it."

Stephanie and I said nothing else. We also were a little concerned that this wasn't the end. Dr. Arora had thought he got it before. How was this time different? At that moment, we had no idea that Dr. Arora's confidence was well placed. He had successfully ablated Samuel and put in a tissue valve. I was mentally preparing to dig back in and fight for the long haul, and suddenly, we had arrived. I went from thinking we would fight on, no matter how long it took, no matter how many times I had to get back up off the mat – to finding out the fight was over.

CHAPTER 12

A VISION REALIZED, ANOTHER BATTLE

"WHEN THE LORD RESTORED THE CAPTIVES OF ZION, WE WERE LIKE DREAMERS. THEN OUR MOUTHS WERE FILLED WITH LAUGHTER AND OUR TONGUES WITH SHOUTS OF JOY. THEN IT WAS PROCLAIMED AMONG THE NATIONS, 'THE LORD HAS DONE GREAT THINGS FOR THEM.'" ~ PSALMS 126:1-2 NASB

It was now May. The late spring rains and early warmth had caused the grass to grow quickly. The grass was a little longer than it should have been, and I needed to mow it. It was a little over a month since Samuel had been released from the hospital.

It took a bit of convincing to get Stephanie outside to our back yard. She was still struggling mentally from the trauma of Samuel's journey, but I finally convinced her to join me.

Samuel took his first steps not long after being released from the hospital. He was over a year and a half old. We were overjoyed that he had finally hit this milestone. He was now starting to scoot around the house quite quickly. I was determined that he was walking fast enough inside. It was now time to see him run outside.

I handed my phone to Stephanie. "Hey babe, will you video this?" I asked. I was excited; this was the moment in my vision. This vision that I had been waiting for so long, seeing Samuel running through the back yard, was here. He could walk, he was healthy, and it was a beautiful sunny day. I was sure this would be it.

Stephanie had no idea what I was doing. After some convincing, she held the phone and waited at the ready to hit record. "Tell me when," she replied.

"Go ahead," I said, excited with anticipation. This moment had been etched in my mind. Samuel was wearing a short-sleeve onesie. His diaper hung out the sides by the snaps, and his white legs were a stark contrast to both his red and blue striped clothing and the dark green grass. He sat on my left arm with his right elbow perched on my shoulder, smiling but unsure of why we were suddenly outside.

Satisfied that Stephanie was ready to video, I attempted to turn Samuel around. The movement startled him, and he would not let go of my neck. He whined, uncertain of the circumstances and not wanting to leave daddy's warm body. The mid-60's temperatures felt amazing to me, but not so much to a toddler.

As I lowered him to the ground, Samuel held his knees to his chest. Unsure of what was happening, he held them there until he could no longer keep them up. My back, weak from not working out, started to ache as I waited for him to extend his legs. I outlasted him, and he eventually lowered his feet to touch the grass. He stood for a moment and took one shaky step before breaking down into tears. He lifted his

Video: Samuel and the water slide
http://www.rlshawver.com/ftcihp-vid5

arms, tears already streaming down his face, asking to be picked up. He didn't like the strange feel of the grass underneath his tiny feet.

I was disappointed; I had been waiting for this event to happen for months. I sighed in frustration as we went back inside. The picture-perfect moment I had hoped for did not happen as I had pictured it would.

However, I wouldn't have to wait long for the fulfilment of the vision. That summer, he was tearing around in the yard as though he had never known any type of illness, his pale skin screaming as loud as him in the bright summer sun.

He always wanted to be shirtless, and his pale body and blond head were a stark contrast to the dark green of our lawn. He and I spent most of our summer evenings and weekends out there. Before long, the scar on his chest and the delay in speech development were the only indicators that he was different from any other toddler.

His running through our yard was a fulfillment of my faith in God's word. His running around outside was a fulfillment of the vision God had planted in my heart in our darkest struggle. Running around our yard was the first full sign that Samuel would live long in the land and grow strong in the land.

Samuel is now six years old. He is tall, strong, and loud. He cares deeply about others and likes to compliment people on their shoes. He is doing quite well despite how much he has been through.

Since Samuel had his last surgery at 18 months old, we have met with Dr. Arora approximately every 6 months. Over time, we noticed that Samuel was less and less energetic. When playing with other kids, he would often sit after running a very short way, which is a strong indication that his heart valve isn't functioning as well.

After four and a half years with a pig valve, it finally needed replaced. We had expected this to happen. Three summers ago, we thought a valve replacement was imminent, and Stephanie and I both panicked. I was heading to a camping trip with some close friends when I heard. Thankfully, I was driving alone, and I was able to pour my rage into my driving and some heavy metal. When I finally calmed down enough to pray about it, the Holy Spirit whispered to me that this surgery will not be like before. Samuel is no longer a baby, and we are no longer fighting SVT. In being able to process this myself, I was also able to help Stephanie process her thoughts and put the situation into proper perspective. Fortunately, it turned out that he only had some sort of flu, and we were able to postpone the surgery for a few more years.

This past summer, as Samuel was getting ready to turn six, Dr. Arora finally decided the old pig valve was no longer sufficient. He suggested that it was time to replace Samuel's valve. While any heart surgery is strenuous, the faith I had developed when Samuel was a baby made this heart surgery significantly different.

We met for Samuel's checkup in late August. Dr. Arora ordered an echo to be performed on Samuel's heart, as was common. This procedure measures the pressure gradient across the valve, and it allows the size of the heart to be measured. We were always glad to see Dr. Arora. His smile and his admiration for Samuel was clearly evident. We met in a small patient room in the back of the Children's Hospital North Campus.

The three of us were wearing masks, and we were worried that the hospital staff would only let one of us in to talk to Dr. Arora. This was in the middle of the COVID lockdown of 2020, and every organization was implementing policies to keep people safe – sometimes at the expense of common sense. Thankfully, there was no restriction on us coming to Samuel's appointment together.

As we walked into the room, immediately to the right was a set of cabinets and a sink. To the left, a small computer desk sat with a large monitor. The walls were a warm color, which contrasted the stark white of the linoleum floor and tile ceiling.

When Dr. Arora eventually entered the room, he came in with his usual swiftness and quick greeting, fixing his eyes and smile on us. As always, he said hello to Stephanie and me, and then to Samuel.

"Samuel, how are you doing buddy?" Dr. Arora asked firmly, attempting to make eye contact. He held out his hand to Samuel for a handshake.

Samuel grunted and squirmed to get out of his gaze, as is common for 5-year-olds. This is especially true when they are nervous.

"Samuel," I said in my dad tone, "stand up straight, say hi, and shake his hand."

He reluctantly did so. Dr. Arora proceeded to ask Samuel about his schooling and what he likes to do for fun, making sure to treat him as an adult. Dr. Arora then turned to Stephanie and me to ask medical questions.

"How are his stamina levels?" Dr. Arora asked. This was a common question at every one of his visits.

"He seems a lot less energetic," Stephanie answered.

I nodded and continued, "He really seems tired and winded after the smallest amount of exercise."

Dr. Arora nodded in response. Since the scare 3 years earlier, we had noticed Samuel's energy levels were slowly declining. He seemed to have much less energy than other children his age, as well as his older brother. Every appointment for the past few years, our response had been pretty much the same – he doesn't seem to have the stamina he had before.

In previous visits, we had come to find out that his fatigue and the stenosis from the valve (increased pressure due to the valve not being large enough) were not the only factor to consider. Dr. Arora and his surgical team had to balance the bad effects a poor valve had on Samuel's health with the problems caused by frequent surgeries. He had undoubtedly described this balance to Stephanie in a visit where I was not able to make it. That day, he explained it to me.

"It's always a balancing act," Dr. Arora explained, "between doing the valve replacement too early and doing it too late and actually causing damage to the heart. Samuel's left side is enlarged from having to make up the difference where the artificial heart valve is too small. We can see that from the X-Rays."

He continued, "At this point, we need to go ahead and schedule the surgery. The big question is whether to put in a mechanical valve or a pig valve. If we do a mechanical valve, you will have to be adamant about keeping his anti-coagulation levels (blood thinners) in check. On the flip side, Samuel's next heart valve replacement could be in his twenties. If we do a pig valve, you could be less strict with his anti-coagulation, but it would probably only last five years."

We nodded, processing what Dr. Arora said. I could tell Stephanie was getting more stressed about the prospects of another surgery. Samuel could sense it, and he started to act out. At the point of mentioning a mechanical valve and having to closely monitor Samuel's blood thinner levels, she tensed more. The tension level in the room grew thick.

Ignoring Samuel's acting out, and us trying to keep him calm, Dr. Arora continued; "We'd like to send him to a hematologist (blood specialist) to make sure he doesn't potentially have a clotting condition."

I was confused by this, "I thought we were sure that the reason Samuel clotted out so many heart valves was because of the SVT."

Dr. Arora quickly shook his head, "Honestly, we don't know. It could have been a clotting condition. It could have been the SVT. We've never before dealt with a case like Samuel's, where a patient had both severe SVT and severe mitral valve 'regurge.'"

I was stunned. I had no idea Samuel was such a rare case.

Dr. Arora continued, "Yes, Samuel baffled us. His case has been heavily studied."

Sometimes it's both exciting and exhausting being unique.

A few weeks later, we made it in to see Samuel's hematologist. He had no concerns about Samuel having clotting issues. That meant a mechanical valve was the wiser route, but the pressure of having to be vigilant about Samuel's blood thinners weighed on Stephanie. I reassured her that she had always done a fantastic job of this. Since Samuel was born, she kept him within the correct range. This is a huge feat, as he was constantly growing, constantly struggling with eating, and constantly changing. There were always factors outside of our control, yet she managed to keep his anti-coagulation levels steady for 6 years. I reassured her that it should only get easier from here as he grows less.

I also had to deal with my own stresses. A few months prior, I had finally found a much less stressful job, a job where my peers and leadership treated me with respect. Despite the positive environment, I was concerned about the off chance that my employers would view me in a negative light for having to deal with this. I also had to make sure the new insurance would cover everything. Thankfully, none of these concerns were problematic. My bosses were exceptionally understanding, and the insurance covered the entire procedure without question, after calling in to get pre-approval.

The other stress was the battle with fear. Once again, this battle was incredibly different from any previous battles.

Forgive me if I personify fear. I believe that there is a personified version of evil, meaning Satan and his demonic forces. I believe he has a plan of attack. The details often change (the who, the what, the how), but the methods are often very similar. In this case, Satan knew he couldn't get me to take hold of my fears through direct confrontation. He knew he had to slide it in slowly and without me noticing. He chose to attack while I was waiting on the Lord, trying to connect with Him.

Despite the realization a few years earlier that this would not be the same, there was still a slight uneasiness in the back of my mind. From late August when surgery was decided, something just felt off.

On September 17th, we heard from Dr. Arora about a scheduling of the surgery. The Hematologist gave us the opinion that Samuel was at no risk of clotting. We would have the surgery at the end of October, exactly one month after Samuel's sixth birthday.

The next point of uneasiness came through my dad. My parents and I were talking on the phone on the Saturday after. Towards the end of the conversation, my dad told me he had a bad feeling about the surgery. While my dad isn't a practicing Christian, he often has accurate premonitions. This caused me more concern.

I wanted to take some time to seek the presence of God about the surgeries. I knew God's promise that Samuel would live long in the land and grow strong in the land were just as true before as they were now. I knew beyond a shadow of a doubt that Samuel would be fine. I wasn't sure of what all preparations I needed to make, and how long this process would go.

However, it was difficult to find a long enough time to fast and pray like I wanted. I had work and family obligations. As during Samuel's earlier surgeries, I had to take time in the morning daily seeking the Lord. Since almost everyone was working from home, including me, I did not have the extra time in the car to process my thoughts and pray. I was able to find a suitable replacement for that time with my daily walks. The early morning reading and the daily walks were the only time I was really getting to seek God's face.

The Holy Spirit hadn't given me any messages about Samuel's surgery since we found out about it, and I wanted the peace and confidence that came with that. I craved that close intimacy and the specific direction that the Holy Spirit gives. I know sometimes the battles can be long, and I wanted to make sure I was in tune with God and did not miss His direction. Having heard nothing from God about this, I did what I knew to do. I fell back on the old messages I had received from God and the truths from the Bible I knew to be accurate. While there was a lot that I had found in my digging through the Bible, and from the things that God had told me in the previous surgeries, my faith had grown soft.

Two days later, in my morning men's group, one of the men from the group wanted to encourage me about the upcoming surgery. I had announced the surgery date that morning, and they all prayed for me over Zoom at the end of our meeting. He called me after and took a few minutes to chat with me on the phone.

When he called, though, he talked about people who had major medical conditions. While these people he spoke of were close to God, these people had never experienced physical healing. God had healed them emotionally, but they continued to live with disabilities and health challenges. I listened intently, but this added more to my fear.

After I got off the phone with him, I was upset. At first, I couldn't pinpoint why. As I turned the conversation over in my head, I began to realize a pattern. I was under attack. Satan was laying a snare for me. He was trying to get me to accept an outcome for Samuel that didn't include him being healthy and whole. This guy wasn't trying to hurt me, or to lead me in the wrong direction. He was trying to encourage me and keep me from being hurt by my expectations. But I knew well that expectations are the evidence of what I am believing.

For better or worse, I called him back an hour later. I tried to be respectful, but I got a little heated. In fact, I got angry.

"Forgive me for being bold," I said, beginning to pace in my back yard, "and I hope I'm not being rude," I continued, "but please don't ever come to someone facing a health challenge and fail to encourage them by telling them of the times when God heals. Don't tell them stories where God didn't show up!"

I continued, still speaking passionately into my phone, "I want to hear stories about how God heals." I proceeded to launch into multiple stories I knew and held dear to me.

"I think about a guy I do business with who had a nerve injury in his leg. It shrank, and he couldn't use it. He couldn't wear pants over top of it, it hurt so bad. He lay on the end of the bed with his leg straight because he couldn't bend it. And God came to him, in the middle of the night. He woke up and his leg was normal size. It didn't hurt. It was bent and touching the floor."

I couldn't stop at this point, "And the stories I hear from mission trips with our church. There was a person who wasn't a preacher, she just chose to go on a mission trip. There was a child who legs were bent, who had club foot. The little boy couldn't walk and couldn't stand. She put her hands on the child's leg, and she began to pray and ask God to heal him. While she was praying, she felt popping and creaking INSIDE OF THE BOY'S LEGS. The child's bones were straightening out underneath his skin as this girl prayed over him. He was able to stand and walk, without a problem."

I continued with a third example, and I apologized again about being so bold.

It was in that moment that I realized I was under attack, but I knew without a doubt that my God, my Heavenly Father, would not let me be put to shame.

Fear didn't give up at that point, though. We had others, leaders in the church who questioned whether God would bring healing to

Samuel. With tears in my eyes, I told them that I would not be put to shame for trusting in God.

When the attacks of fear through leaders and elders didn't work, Satan continued to try to slip in his attacks by whispering scary events while I was walking, or one of the few times I wasn't active. Unlike when Samuel went through his first surgery, I was well seasoned at this type of warfare.

When I would walk at lunch, fear would constantly try to slip images into my head. I didn't respond. I really didn't care what fear had to say. As time wore on, I wanted fear to think it was getting the upper hand. I was baiting fear. It continued day after day, but my mood didn't change. My attitude didn't change. I knew exactly what I expected. As the surgery date grew closer, fear became more active at trying to woo me. The voice of fear spoke to me in the mornings and in the evenings. It seemed oblivious that I wasn't affected. I knew Samuel was going to come through surgery without a hitch, if God didn't do the bigger miracle and make his heart valve whole.

Day after day, for almost two weeks, the thoughts in my head would speak fear. I never responded. The visions and images would come, and I kept quiet.

One overcast day a few weeks before the surgery, I finally had enough. Another image popped in my head as I was walking at lunch, and I addressed fear directly, "Fear, my God will not fail me. Samuel will live long in the land and grow strong in the land. He's going to come through this surgery perfectly fine."

Immediately after speaking that confession out loud, fear left. The images and voices did not come back. I would have welcomed it – to beat it over the head with God's word and my faith. The Bible calls

God's word a weapon, and I had become proficient using it.

For the next few weeks, time passed as though we were waiting for a doctor's appointment, not open-heart surgery. I was working from home, so Stephanie and both boys were getting lots of my attention.

A week before the surgery, anxiety started to hit when they had Samuel come into the hospital. They brought him in to show him what was going to happen on the day of the surgery, and the various rooms he would be in at each step of the process. Because of the Covid-19 lockdowns, they weren't allowed to take Samuel through to show him in person. Instead, they showed him pictures.

The pictures triggered a lot of stress in Stephanie and me. We had seen each of those rooms so many times when Samuel was younger. Samuel responded to our stress and began acting out in the exam office. This made Stephanie and I more stressed, until I finally realized what was happening and took measures to calm all of us.

Video: Playing Pranks
http://www.rlshawver.com/ftcihp-vid6

The day of surgery arrived, and the surgery itself went off without a hitch. Samuel stayed in the hospital a total of 6 days. While there, Stephanie and I used the opportunity to lift up other people in encouragement and prayer. We alternated nights staying with him. The day after surgery, the occupational therapist had Samuel out of bed and walking around the hospital. We were in the hospital through Halloween, and we spent the day pranking people.

Samuel continued recovering at a rapid pace. His first week home, he spent hunched over, afraid he would hurt his chest if he stood up straight. He kept his head cocked to his left side, as he was still hurting from the PICC line that was in his neck. By the end of the second week, he no longer favored his neck. By the end of the third week, he was no longer slouching. We took him

Video: Samuel Dancing
http://www.rlshawver.com/ftcihp-vid7

and another friend's daughter to Dave and Buster's exactly three weeks after Samuel's surgery, and he danced as though no one was watching. But everyone will be watching because I have the video.

Samuel running around our yard was the fulfillment of the vision God gave me, but I'm still living out the fulfillment of my faith for him. God promised that the children of the righteous will grow strong in the land, and I will remind God of that every time someone or something threatens my son's life. The Bible says that God loves to be reminded of His promises. The fulfillment of my faith is Samuel living to a ripe old age of over 100.

I pray my story has been an encouragement to you, and that you find ways to win your battles using faith as your weapon. Go and knock down all the gates of hell you find. I pray God's blessing of His presence with you, and that you seek it diligently. Go and find out what the feeling of His presence is like. I pray that you see miracles bigger and bolder than I've experienced, and that you get to see them as the fulfillment of your faith. Stand on His word – there is nothing else.

And lastly, I pray that, through the righteousness that comes from your faith in Jesus, your children will live long in the land and grow strong in the land.

GRATITUDE

I first off want to give all credit and glory where it is due - nothing in this book would be possible without my Heavenly Father, the sacrifice of His Son Jesus, and the presence and guidance of His Holy Spirit. His goodness and mercy have followed me and have been an ever-present help in my life.

Second, I want to give a huge thanks to my mentor through all of this, Jake Baker. He mentored me and prayed with me and for me from the time we found out Samuel was having his first heart surgery. He counselled me on how to stand in faith at every turn. Had he not led me in the way he did, I don't know if Samuel would be alive. I don't know if my marriage would have stayed together. I don't know if I would have mentally been able to handle any of it.

Third, I want to give a huge thank you to my wife, Stephanie. What she did taking care of Samuel, being there by his side every minute he was in the hospital, was the most beautiful picture of a mother's love I have ever seen. It's also a lovely picture of God's gentle nature. She doesn't see the significance of it nearly enough, but she gave everything she had to my son. I am so incredibly proud of her.

Fourth, I want to give a huge thanks to all the people who visited us and were there for us. Stephanie's parents, Edith and John, and Stephanie's sister Zoi. They were there for us, behind the scenes, helping us stay afloat mentally, spiritually, and practically.

Dane and Karen Taylor, who were always just there. Their example showed us that sometimes just showing up is the most important thing you can do. Sometimes saying nothing is the best thing to say.

Mom, Dad, thank you for making the long trips up to be there when you could.

Mike, Shru, Kyle, Aaron and Olesea, Liz, Pastor Chris, Jan, Julie, Brian, and Toni, and so many other friends - thank you for visiting, for bringing food, for just being there.

Gabby, thanks for being hospital buddies with us, you have a great story too.

Fifth, to my editing team, you guys floor me. Thank you, Matt Chatham, who returned the book with comments to me in four days. Thank you, Alex Berry for reading my third and fourth drafts and helping me clarify what I want to say. Thank you also to Sabrina Richardson, Debbie Kortyna, Josh Kaufmann, Denise Cattley, and my mom; thank you for all of your edits and your opinions. They are very much welcomed.

Sixth, to every single person who said even one prayer for us, thank you from the bottom of our hearts. You held up the reigns of prayer when we couldn't, or were too tired, or didn't know what to say. You agreed with us for his healing and our safety. You were fellow petitioners of our loving God. To those who prayed daily, wow. You guys are amazing. Thank you.

HOW TO HAVE A RELATIONSHIP WITH GOD

First, I'm not a minister and I don't have a seminary degree. I'm really just a big dude with a big smile who's been fortunate enough to be mentored by some pretty great people, people who have continuously pointed me towards God. The good news is that God's not in the habit of checking pedigrees – He's in the habits of checking hearts. That's where I want to talk to you from today.

What's the point of all this Jesus stuff? Does He really do miracles? Can I really trust Him to do miracles today? There is a plethora of questions I'm sure you could be asking right now – but I want to share my perspective with you.

I'll start with the first hypothetical question I imagine you must be thinking – what's the point of all this Jesus stuff? God created you in His image. He designed you so that He could know you and you could know Him. He replicated this same relationship structure in in healthy marriages and in healthy parent-child relationships and in healthy friendships. Mind you, I want to stress the healthy part. He wants to have that same level of fantastic, healthy relationship with you.

To do that, it's going to mean turning from a life lead by yourself and your desires, away from what God calls sin, and turn to a life of relationship with God.

To the second question, does God really do miracles today? Yes, he very much does. But let me ask you a question, do you really need me to tell you that to not see it. When you look at your own life, at the delicate balance of the universe, the solar system, or the eco system – do these not scream wildly that there's someone behind the scenes keeping it all in balance. When you see that the atom is created in the image of the solar system, or that a completely new life can be created from two separate people, a feat no scientist no matter how brilliant has ever accomplished? Do these things not make you think that maybe there is something more than just living and dying?

At this point, I want to offer you the opportunity to have a relationship with God. If you are praying for a miracle for your child or loved one, I want to invite you to get to get to know God. I want you to call him the God of the miraculous, but in all honesty, His reality is simply not ours.

To begin with, there's one thing that separates you and God – your sin.

Before you start weighing the cost of becoming perfect, let me tell you that is impossible.

So logically, not being separated from God is impossible. Yes, technically, you are correct. That's why you need a miracle. God sent His only son, Jesus, to become a man on earth 2,000 years ago. He died on the cross as a miraculous sacrifice to remove the legal guilt of all of your sins. He then did another miracle and rose from the grave.

Here's one more miracle to add to that list – that sacrifice is available to you. I want to invite you, humbly, to accept this as truth and to say this prayer.

"God, I am a sinner.

"You gave your son to die for me on the cross, 2,000 years ago to take my sins. Today, I turn from my sins to You and Him. Forgive me, cleanse me of all my sins, and make me whole. Today, I accept Jesus as my Lord and Savior. I ask you to fill me with your Holy Spirit.

"In Jesus name, Amen."

If you prayed that prayer, and you have chosen to turn your life to God, congratulations. You have made the most important decision in your life. You are no longer a sinner; you are literally now a part of the body of Christ. Welcome.

From here, I give you three more instructions:

1. Tell someone you know is a Christian that you are a Christian. If you don't know anyone, or you would rather tell me, then email me here, at RONALD_SHAWVER@HOTMAIL.COM or use the QR code below. I would love that:

2. Grab a Bible and start reading it regularly. A fantastic starting point is the book of John. You don't have to read a ton. If you can't afford a Bible, email me and I will send you one. There is also a great app called the Bible app by Life. Church, where you can download the Bible and have it directly on your phone.

3. Find a church in your area that believes in Jesus and the Bible and in modern day miracles. Feel free to email me and I will be glad to assist in helping you find one.

4. Get baptized. Baptism is an outward public declaration that you are now a follower of Jesus. It doesn't make you saved – it's an act of obedience to God.

THANK YOU AND RESOURCES

I appreciate you reading our story. This has been a labor of love - sharing my heart and pains and victories. I hope that you are coming more and more to realize this: because of Jesus, we have authority through Him over sickness and even death. It is my desire that I have inspired you to take a bold stand on what you know is right and to understand the good that God wants for your life.

To keep up with myself, Samuel, Izaiah, and of course my beautiful wife Steph, check us out on our webpage: www.rlshawver.com, or with the QR code at the right.

You can also follow us at Facebook, by looking up "For this Child I Have Prayed – Samuel's Medical story", or by going to QR code at the left.

Also, you can follow things here for more resources, including scripture verses to declare over your child or groups who can help.

https://rlshawver.com/for-this-child-i-have-prayed/resources